MAKING HIM *Loyal*

How Christian women who do it "the right way" end up bitter and broken

BY KAREN C. DAVIS

Making Him Loyal: How Christian women who do it "the right way" end up bitter and broken

Copyright © 2022 by Karen C. Davis. All Rights Reserved.
Published by Focus Enterprises Publications, an imprint of Focus Integrative Healthcare LLC.

No part of this book may be reproduced or transmitted, downloaded, distributed, reverse engineered, or stored in or introduced into any information storage and retrieval system, in any form or by any means, including photocopying and recording, whether electronic or mechanical, now known or hereinafter invented without permission in writing from the publisher.

Publisher's Cataloging-in-Publication data
Names: Davis, Karen Charlene, author.
Title: Making him loyal : how Christian women who do it "the right way" end up bitter and broken / Karen C. Davis.
Description: Atlanta, GA: Focus Enterprises Publications, 2022.
Identifiers: LCCN: 2021925569 | ISBN: 9780998350141
Subjects: LCSH Davis, Karen C. | Marriage. | Marriage--Religious aspects--Christianity. | Christian life. | BISAC BIOGRAPHY & AUTOBIOGRAPHY / Personal Memoirs | RELIGION / Christian Living / Love & Marriage | FAMILY & RELATIONSHIPS / Dating
Classification: LCC BV835 .D38 2022 | DDC 248.8/44/092--dc23

MAKING HIM *Loyal*

CONTENTS

Dedication ... vi
Introduction ... ix
Chapter 1. The Broken Picture ... 1
Chapter 2. Meeting Mark ... 7
Chapter 3. An Omen, a Premonition, a Sign! ... 13
Chapter 4. Sporting With Each Other ... 19
Chapter 5. Falling Short of the Ideal ... 25
Chapter 6. Remolding Mark ... 33
Chapter 7. The Transformation ... 39
Chapter 8. Revelations of Infidelity ... 45
Chapter 9. The Confrontation ... 53
Chapter 10. The Separation ... 61
Chapter 11. In Clandestine Places ... 69
Chapter 12. His Mighty Hands ... 77
Chapter 13. Authentic vs Inauthentic Repentance ... 85
Chapter 14. Off the Deep End ... 95
Chapter 15. Fight or Flight ... 101
Chapter 16. Out of the Miry Clay ... 109
Chapter 17. Pressing Toward the Mark ... 115
Chapter 18. On Higher Ground ... 125

DEDICATION

This book is dedicated to my children, Jerell, Janelle, and Jersel.

I will never forget the day I looked back and saw you marching behind me, repeating my chant. That was the moment I knew I had to persevere. I had to keep fighting. I had to push myself to recovery for me, for you, for God!

THANKS TO...

God, who tarried with me through it all and beautifully turned my mess into a message.

***

My husband, Dan. You have been my support and inspiration. You brought a beautiful resolution to my story.

INTRODUCTION

ARE YOU HURTING? HAVE you been betrayed by someone you love? Are you at this moment going through life feeling empty, rejected, and forlorn? In this book, I bring you hope. I want you to know that amid the storms that so often weather our lives, there is hope. If you look deep enough, you will see a flicker of light at the end of the tunnel. In our difficult moments and experiences, we may see darkness all around. There seems to be no way out. The hurt, the pain, and the sadness sometimes cloud the light without, and we grope through life feeling alone and abandoned by God. We ask questions such as: Why? Why me? How could this happen to me? What did I do to deserve this? If you are going through a difficult experience, and you feel like giving up, you are in the right place with the right book in hand.

The experiences in this book are true, and it shows the guiding hands of God in our difficult moments. In my difficult moments, I felt hopeless and helpless. I did not want to live anymore because the burden was too heavy to bear. I felt abandoned by God and questioned His love for me. I screamed at Him, for I could not understand why I lived according to His word, and yet, He turned His back on me. Thank God, He spared my life to see that I was not alone. I was never alone! He was right there with me through it all. As you go through your difficult moments, I want you to know that He is right there with you, too. It may seem as though He has abandoned you, but be patient because He hasn't! He never does! He is touched by your aching heart. Give yourself a chance, and you will make it through your difficult moments as a stronger and better person. Never give up. There is a better day coming!

In this book, you will become privy to the devastating and debilitating effects of infidelity. Many do not know, neither can they fathom what victims of infidelity go through. In these pages, I allow you to step into my life and get into my mind and see for yourself its devasting and debilitating effects. It is by far one of the most degrading and defeating experience an individual can go through. It leaves you feeling inadequate, unattractive, and worthless. Being a victim of infidelity, I felt defeated and rejected. Each day, I experienced chronic feelings of emptiness and feelings of emotional numbness and despair. I was a kite giving way to the restless wind. I was going down. I was a car spinning out of control about to crash. If you are a victim of infidelity, and you feel inadequate and worthless, I want you to know that you do not have to feel that way. You are special, special in the eyes of God. Never for one moment think that your spouse cheated because something is wrong with you. NOTHING IS WRONG WITH YOU! People cheat because something is wrong with them!

At the time I was going through these experiences, I could not see beyond the hurt and the pain I was experiencing. I developed a "woe is me" mentality and found myself in a pit of despair. I can look back now and see that God was giving me a testimony. I believe that He authored my story and placed it in my possession so that I can share it with you and give you hope, hope of a better life ahead. You must never give up when difficulties come your way or crumble in the face of adversity. You can always find your strength in God. He may not show up when you want him to, but you can trust Him to work things out for you in His time. Ask Him for the strength to make it through. Put your hands in His, and He will walk with you each step of the way. May the words of this book bring solace to your heart as you behold the miraculous workings of His hands.

One

THE BROKEN PICTURE

BY NOW I HAD the gut feeling that Mark was having an affair. I could see so many signs. The late nights, the condoms hidden in our car, and the sexually revealing marks on his neck, all hinted that something was brewing. Each time I confronted Mark, he had an excuse. He claimed that the marks on his neck came from a chemical he uses to wash the car, and that the condoms were planted by people seeking to break up our marriage. Mark was the author of excuses. He became a professional and pathological liar, and my life became a mixture of hurt, pain, and tears. Each time I returned home from work, I became depressed. The only place I found comfort was at church. There I got encouragement to make it through. I tried hard to hide my depression from my church family, yet some detected the sadness in my eyes. A hug, a shake of the hand, a prayer, all managed to temporarily lift my spirits. I went to church every weekend, attended prayer meetings during the week, and yet I felt alone and abandoned by God.

One Sunday evening, I sat in my living room in tears. I laid my head in my arms and cried. I felt like I could not go on any further. I was confused. I wanted to believe that it was all in my imagination. I wanted to believe all Mark's excuses. I cried, and I cried. I reflected on our courtship and the first three years of our marriage. I was happy. Now my life was turned up-side-down. I was the epitome of sadness and grief. I lifted my head for a moment and with tears streaming down my face, I glanced at the picture on the wall. It was a picture of Mark and me in our happy days. I laid my head back and allowed my mind to wander back to those happy days, days filled with joy, laughter, and comradery. Mark was my knight in shining armor, everything I wanted in a man! He was fun-loving, entertaining, and charming. His presence lit up a room and brought joy and laughter to everyone around. He was comical in every sense of the word, and I loved being around him, for he brought an inexplicable happiness to my life. He was that special someone I dreamed would come into my life and fill it with memories, satisfaction, and anticipation. He was my significant other, my best friend. For the three years of courtship and the first three years of marriage, our love seemed unique. We talked for hours and never got weary of each other. We spent memorable times together and valued every moment in each other's presence. He bought me gifts and made me laugh. He opened doors and pulled out chairs for me. He was the perfect gentleman, every woman's dream! I was a queen, his queen. In fact, I felt like I was experiencing a bit of heaven on earth. I was totally happy, and he seemed happy, too. I was so pleased with the man I had chosen. He was my soulmate, God's gift to me.

Now everything had taken a downward slide. Never in my wildest dream did I envision that this would be my fate. Growing up, I thought myself destined for a perfect life— a life filled with joy and happiness. After all, I was gentle, kind, affectionate, and thoughtful. I followed biblical principles, and most importantly, I stayed away from pre-marital sex. These attributes I thought would guarantee me a life of eternal bliss. In fact, He had promised to deliver me from all evil if I lived by His word. "Because he hath set his love upon me, therefore will I deliver him: I will set him on high, because he hath known my name. He shall call upon me, and I will answer him: I will be with him in trouble; I will deliver him, and honour him" (Psalms 91: 14-15). Sadly, I was young and did not yet understand that in this sinful world, difficulties and disappointments are bound to come our way. God may not directly cause these difficulties, but He sometimes allows them. If or when they come our way, we must ask Him to give us the discernment to understand why they happened and how they can benefit our lives. The scripture teaches us that "... all things work together for good to them that love God, to them who are the called according to his purpose" (Rom 8: 28).

My eyes rested on the picture once again. I had placed the picture of Mark and me on the wall as a concrete embodiment of the love we shared: the closeness, the security, the happiness. This portrait, so deeply cherished, had hung majestically in the same spot, untouched, in our living room for about three years as a symbol of our devotion and love. We took this picture at the onset of our relationship, so it hung on the wall as a constant reminder of a friendship that grew and blossomed into a bravura love affair. The more I stared at the picture, the more the tears spouted from my eyes. I placed my head in my arms once again and sobbed. The room was still. In its stillness, one could hear a pin drop.

Suddenly, there was a loud noise and the sound of breaking glass. I jumped. My heart leaped and began to race! What could that be? It sounded so near, yet I could not detect exactly what made the noise. My eyes glanced at the wall, and a strange blank space stared back at me. Something was missing! I jumped up and gazed at the floor. Lying to the side of the chair was a mass of shattered glass. Out of nowhere, our picture that had stood in its place for about three years, without any movement, without any help, simply removed itself from the wall, crashed to the floor, and smashed into pieces. I stared at the heap before me. I was horrified. Once again, I lifted my eyes to the wall to make sure I was not imagining, but no, I was not. Our picture, our symbol, our embodiment of love mysteriously fell to the ground and smashed into pieces. Was this a sign? Was this the end of a relationship that I thought would last forever?

I cried more and more. The tears cascaded down my face and dripped onto the heap of broken glass below me. I wanted to believe this was not a sign, yet in my heart I sensed it was. *Oh God in heaven, help me,* was the grief-stricken cry of my soul. I cried, and I cried. I pondered on the shattered glass before me and made a hurtful connection to my sad state of affairs. My relationship with Mark was over. I just knew it! Our bond was broken.

In sadness, I made my way back to the chair. Never in my wildest dream did I envision such sad turn of events. I laid my head back on the chair and wept. My heart was broken. My soul was aching. I felt abandoned. Where was God when I needed Him most? He had promised to be with me in times of trouble and in times of woe, and He did not keep His word. I had set my love upon Him, yet in my troubles, my trials, and my tribulations, He did not deliver me. I got up and stared at the shattered portrait once again. I felt crushed. I wanted to believe I was wrong. I wanted to believe it was all in my imagination, yet in my heart, I knew it was true. My marriage to Mark was over. My hope, my dreams, and my aspirations had all fallen to naught. I sat back down. I could not stop the tears from flowing. As I contemplated the shattered glass, the broken picture, and the sad turn of events, I felt empty, rejected, and forlorn. I laid my head back on the chair, and I wept.

Two

MEETING MARK

HOW DID WE GET to this point? I stretch my mind, and I go back to the days when I first met Mark. We first met at a youth camp when I was 18 and he was 20. It was a five-day sleep over camp where young people got together annually to have fun and fellowship. At camp, we would have numerous engaging activities, the best of which were spending time at the beach and making new friends. The nightly pranks to annoy each other, the talent-filled performances, and the facetious behaviors accentuated the entertainment already taking place. At these annual camps, lasting bonds were established, many of which blossomed into life-long commitments. Attending religiously since I was 14 years old, each year I looked forward to them because they were inspiring, engaging, and memorable.

Some friends and I were hanging out together at the campsite one afternoon when Mark and some friends approached us and introduced themselves.

"How are you all doing?" Joe asked.

"We're doing well," we seemed to answer in unison.

"You all look lost to me!" Mark chimed in. Immediately, they engaged us in conversation. They seemed to be very friendly and respectful guys, so we did not cease to entertain their jovial conversations. Although their jokes were quite corny, they were fun to be around. I spoke to Mark many times during the five-day camp but saw him only as a new-found friend. By the end of the camp, I had acquired some meaningful relationships, not just with Mark and his friends, but with all the attendees, and I left the camp with a promise to stay in touch.

Months later, I ran into Mark at a religious conference that was being held over the course of one month. I visited regularly and found myself talking more and more to him. I noticed things about him that I liked. Many young people were attending the conference for the sole purpose of socializing, but not Mark. He was stationed at his seat, listening intently to the speaker, and taking notes. I sat behind him, and ironically, I was taking notes too. I was observing him and thinking about how different he was. Each night when the meeting ended, I would walk over to him and strike up conversations about the speaker's presentation. Mark was very much into what was being presented. I found myself at the conference night after night, and over the course of time, Mark and I became friends, good friends. Finally, he visited my home, and I introduced him to my parents. I visited his home, and he introduced me to his parents. We then went headlong into a courtship that lasted three years.

During our relationship, Mark and I did some unusual things together. When most couples went to the club or the movies, we hung out in parks where we read and studied together. We spent most of our time in nature where we basked in the sunshine of each other's love, enjoying each other's presence. Sex was not on our agenda, for Mark understood that I had made a commitment to abstain from sexual intimacy until marriage. Do not get me wrong! I am not saying that I did not have sexual desires, but I put forth every effort to contain those desires. Mark respected my wish to reserve myself for that special someone who would one day be my husband. Apart from the potential risk of acquiring a sexually transmitted disease, and the emotional damage that could result from a potential break up, I saw obedience to God as an important reason for abstinence. "Flee fornication. Every sin that a man doeth is without the body; but he that committeth fornication sinneth against his own body" (1 Cor 6: 18). I strongly believed that sex outside of the marriage relationship could lead to distrust and guilt if the relationship did not work out. Understanding that it is sometimes difficult to eradicate the emotions attached to early sexual encounters, I feared that I would carry a load of guilt for a long period of time if I gave up something so sacred to someone in passing. When guilt permeates, the joy of a pure sexual experience between husband and wife is clouded, so to foster purity in our relationship, Mark and I made the decision to wait. It increased my self-esteem to know that I was worth the wait, and as a result, our relationship was strengthened. By waiting, we hoped to build the perfect relationship where we would learn to trust and respect each other in a more meaningful way.

    I must confess that there were a few other reasons why I chose to abstain. One reason was fear. Being a Christian youth, I had been to numerous conferences on pre-marital sex, which, as I look back, I now believe left me traumatized. I remember distinctly one night the speaker was presenting on the topic, "Sex and the Single Girl." In an effort to drive home the point of abstinence, he banged the podium, stared into the audience, and uttered, "Young girls, the first experience of sex is bloody and painful! You will remember this experience for the rest of your life, and you do not want to look around, and that person is long gone!" There was a moment of silence. Then he banged the podium once again and yelled, "BLOODY AND PAINFUL!" I cringed in my seat. Without realizing it, I had unconsciously developed a fear of sex. Another reason for wanting to abstain stemmed from my upbringing. Abstinence was an unspoken moral value in my upbringing. We learned about it in our youth group at church, and we understood that it was a value our mom wanted her children to uphold. I did not want to disappoint my mom. She meant the world to me and letting her down would be devastating. Mark was not raised with these values, but had gotten baptized two years prior to meeting me, so he understood and accepted the values with which I was raised. He was also very understanding of the fear I harbored and tried his best to make me feel comfortable and at ease in his presence.

It is not my intention to paint a picture of perfection in our courtship. Like all couples, we had our ups and our downs, but we established a unique friendship that brought us through each obstacle we encountered and helped us survive the problems that we faced. Mark was a self-employed tradesman and was often out of work. I was gainfully employed in a reputable company and many times was left with no choice but to handle the finances on dates. Oftentimes when we went out to eat, I footed the bill. When we went shopping, I bought the clothes. There were times when Mark was out of money, and I supplied him with enough to see him through. Was Mark bothered by this reverse role? I am not sure. Whenever the topic of work came up, he would usually say that work was momentarily slow. He worked occasionally but not regularly.

These financial issues can have serious effects on relationships, but Mark and I ignored them. I saw the problem as temporary and comforted myself with the thought that if Mark had the money, he would do better. I loved him, and that was all that mattered. However, it would have benefited us to take a more mature and level-headed view of the situation. What if Mark was lazy and really had no intention of finding a steady job? What if he was the type of guy who would comfortably sit back and watch me drain myself trying to provide for our family while he contributed little or nothing to manage our home? Would I be able to cope? Would such a situation sever our relationship? Without addressing these issues, I accepted Mark's proposal to get married. With the approval of our parents, we made plans for our big day. In preparation for the big day ahead, we rented an apartment and furnished it. We looked forward to the soon-to-be day when we would walk down the aisle together, then move into our furnished apartment, and be with each other forever.

Three

AN OMEN, A PREMONITION, A SIGN!

IT WAS THE DAY before our wedding. I got up with itchy eyes but passed it off as a simple eye irritation. With each passing moment the itching got more and more severe. I was flabbergasted. This could not be. *Why? Why? Why today of all days?* I was coming down with a pinkeye! Pinkeye results from inflammation of the conjunctiva and is usually linked to bacterial or viral infections. The itchiness began in one eye, and before I knew it, spread to the other. A liquid was constantly leaking from my eyes, and the more I wiped and rubbed my eyes, the puffier they became. I looked in the mirror and cried and cried. I thought about the day ahead. This was supposed to be the biggest event of my life. The more I looked in the mirror, the more I became horrified. My eyes were swollen, puffy, and red. My face looked swollen, too. Each time I looked in the mirror, I became depressed, and each time I called Mark to give him the updates. Crying was not helping the situation and may have caused my eyes to swell even more. Putting off the wedding was not an option. There was no way I could get the word out to every invited guest that the wedding was postponed. To top it all off, I had family that flew in from out of the country. There was no way, definitely no way I could break the news to them that their journey this far was all in vain.

The average woman dreams about a perfect wedding day when, like a queen, she will walk down the aisle in fine garb and perfect splendor to meet her king. From a tender age, she fantasizes about that glorious day when, as she walks down the aisle, everyone stands and serenades her and compliments her for her flawless and matchless beauty. Everything must be perfect. She must be perfect. I looked in the mirror and was devastated. My eyes protruded their sockets, and I almost looked like a different person. I looked as if I had been stung by a bee and was allergic. That dream of a perfect wedding day where I looked my perfect best seemed to be snatched away from me in an instant. *Why did I have to get pinkeye the day before my wedding? How will I walk down the aisle looking like this?* I hated the very thought of it! My face looked horrible. I wished I could awake to realize it was just an awful dream.

I awoke on Sunday morning and hurried to the mirror hoping for a miracle! My face and eyes still looked swollen, and my eyes now looked deep red. However, I decided to face the crowd anyway. I consoled myself with the thought that my love for Mark was greater than the embarrassment of walking down the aisle with a swollen face and eyes leaking puss. As a matter of fact, I decided I was going to hold my head up and proudly walk down the aisle. This was our day, and nothing would come in the way of us being together, not even a swollen face and reddened eyes. I was going to get married to Mark regardless of the unfortunate situation in which I now found myself. Not only did we have a commitment to fulfill, but a lot of money was invested into the wedding that I was not prepared to throw away.

I tried to stop crying and do all that I had to do in preparation for the wedding. I assisted in folding wedding cake to-go boxes. I worked on folding programs and conversed by phone with the decorating team at the reception hall and at the church. Everything was coming together nicely except that the pinkeye was not improving. My face was still swollen, and my eyes looked red. The time for the wedding crept upon me, and I dressed and tried to look my very best. I had a beautifully designed white dress enhanced with lace insertions. Its detachable train and matching veil added splendor to the design. The lovely bridal shoe adorned with seed pearls and the beautifully designed bouquet complemented each other. My hair was nicely combed with a bang falling down my forehead. Neighbors waved from a distance as I stepped into the waiting car. I was leaving my parents' home and stepping into the world of adulthood. I was happy but a little nervous.

Was I really ready for this? Mark and I were so young. Did we really assess the difficulties that could come our way? Were we mature enough to stand with each other through thick and thin, for better, for worse, for richer, for poorer, in sickness and in health, till death? Ask me one hundred times, and I would have told you, yes, we were ready. We loved each other dearly; we received counseling from our pastor; and now we were ready to commit and declare before God, our family, and our friends that we would let nothing, and no one come between us. Throughout our courtship, we had promised to accept each other's differences and encourage each other's individuality. We even promised that when we got married, we would help each other aspire to our fullest potential, and most importantly, we would become one with each other and be one with God. We felt sure that we were on the right path, God's path. We felt ready. This was the best thing that had ever happened to us. The car drove away, and as it drove away, it dawned on me that there was no turning back. I was saying goodbye to my parents' home with the intention that I was never coming back. The closer I got to the church, the more nervous I became. Soon we were at the church. I looked in the handheld mirror once again, and my eyes were still swollen and red.

I stepped out of the bridal car with the determination that I was going to walk down the aisle in style, come what may. I was not going to let pinkeye ruin my long-anticipated day. The wedding started, and the bridal party made their grand entrance into the sanctuary. They looked lovely in their attire. We had practiced four days prior, and I was confident that they would make a perfect entrance. Finally, it was my turn to walk down the aisle. My brother was taking me down the aisle to meet Mark. I clutched him tightly. In my insecurity,

I yearned for some form of security. I stood in the doorway and inspected the crowd before me.

The music began to play, and the attendees stood up awaiting the arrival of the lovely bride. I thought about my dream of a perfect wedding day when, like a queen, I would walk down the aisle in fine garb and perfect splendor to meet my king. I looked at the crowd as they stood ready to serenade me and compliment me for my flawless and matchless beauty. My heart began to beat fast then faster. I took one step then another. As I walked down the aisle, I could feel eyes penetrating me. I read into the stares that met me, stares that seemed to say, "Really…Did she really? Did she really come here with a swollen face and reddened eyes?"

SWOLLEN FACE AND REDDENED EYES. Was this an omen, a premonition, a sign?

Four

SPORTING WITH EACH OTHER

"AND IT CAME TO pass, when he had been there a long time, that Abimelech king of the Philistines looked out at a window, and saw, and behold, Isaac was sporting with Rebekah his wife" (Gen 26: 8). The Greek word translated as sporting means to laugh, play, or joke. Isaac and Rebecca must have been joking and playing and enjoying each other when King Abimelech saw them. Isaac had just made the false claim that Rebekah was his sister. When Abimelech looked out of the window and saw them, he knew right away that they were not brother and sister but husband and wife. They were laughing, joking, and playing with each other in a more intimate way than brothers and sisters do. Maybe they were holding hands, looking into each other's eyes, leaning on each other's shoulders, or giving each other a passionate kiss. So intimate was their behavior that it caused the king to take notice.

That was Mark and I as we stepped into married life. We were like best friends, and everyone could sense it. We "sported" with each other. I remember during our honeymoon, we were sitting in a restaurant, looking into each other's eyes, and enjoying each other when we noticed three women staring at us. As they scrutinized us, we heard them whisper, "Two babies got married." We looked at them and smiled. At first glance, you might mistake us for a brother and sister, but it would not take you long to grasp the intimate connection we shared. Mark and I were always joking, playing, laughing, and having a good time together. You could tell we loved each other by the glow in our eyes. He was slender, but I detected great strength in him. I could be myself, communicate honestly, and never feel judged or criticized by him. I felt secure and protected in his arms, and when I laid in his arms, nothing else mattered. I felt safe.

Husbands and wives were meant to complement each other, and we felt sure that we did. We made each other better by encouraging and pushing each other to our fullest potential. I always believed that a way of demonstrating true love is to help your partner grow. My compliments to Mark on how well he could expound the Bible boosted his confidence to preach and conduct Bible studies, and the more he did it, the better he became. He viewed me as smart and rhetorically gifted, and this boosted my confidence to do talks in church. I encouraged him to keep running long distance races because I saw a future in it for him, and he encouraged me to go into business because he saw a future in it for me. We had promised to never put each other down but rather to build each other up by challenging each other to be better.

We also agreed on the same values and had similar mindsets. We both vowed to keep God at the center of our relationship and in the center of our home. Our belief that God is ever present and sees all that we do reminded us that we needed to treat each other right and treat each other with utmost respect. Hanging in our dining area was a plaque that read, "God is the head of this house. The unseen guest at every meal, the silent listener to every conversation." Knowing that in our sinful state mortal beings are incapable of manifesting the unconditional love that is required in marriage, we understood that to have a successful marriage, we must solicit the help of God. God knows that in and of ourselves it is impossible to love unconditionally, but He invites us to come to Him, lean on Him, and allow His unconditional love to spill over into our hearts and minds.

Soon after our wedding, Mark and I settled into a church near our apartment and became devout members. It did not take us long to become actively involved leaders in the church. At church, we assisted in the adult and youth departments. Mark was preaching, and I was teaching. We were grateful that we could use our God-appointed gifts in His service. We looked forward to weekends, so we could fellowship with our new friends. This gave us a chance to grow in our faith, learn from others, and share what we knew with them. After the youth program in the evening, we would return home exhausted, but we did not hesitate to spend intimate time together. We spent hours talking, joking, and enjoying each other. We couldn't get enough of each other. During the week, we reserved time to read and discuss the Bible so that as a couple we could be equipped and ready to share God's word. "But sanctify the Lord God in your hearts: and *be* ready always to *give* an answer to every man that asketh you a reason of the hope that is in you with meekness and fear" (1 Pet 3:15). Mark was always preparing himself for a Bible study. Anyone who knocked on our door with the intention of discussing the Bible was given a free pass to enter our home. Mark just loved religious discussions.

Additionally, Mark loved sports, and I was beginning to love sports, too. As a couple, we attended soccer games, cricket matches, basketball games, field days, and marathons. Mark was a runner. He was very good with long distance races and embraced every opportunity for competition. We, along with our friends from church, attended numerous sporting events together, and Mark was always the one to brighten up the day. I remember one time while we were at a field day, Mark boasted to everyone that he would win a race. The race began, and Mark was lagging. Everyone looked on with laughter. When the race ended, Mark refused to drop out the race but kept running until he got to the finished line. Everyone fell out laughing. Mark returned with a grin on his face and started preaching: "The race is not for the swift," he said, "but he who endures to the end." Everyone laughed. "The Christian life is not a sprint. It is a marathon," he continued. "We must press towards the mark, keeping our eyes on the prize! The quickness does not matter. It is the endurance that counts!" Mark was a funny guy, and his humor drew people to him.

Mark and I understood that inviting God into our home and into our lives was a key component in preserving our happiness and making our marriage work, so we committed to strengthening our relationship with God. Couples seeking to strengthen their relationship with God devote time to prayer, Bible study, and fellowship. This we did. Prayer opens your heart to God, and allows you to make requests that bless, unify, and strengthen your marriage. There is great reward when couples pray for one another, pray over their concerns, and praise God together as one. Bible study also plays an integral role in strengthening the marriage relationship, for it fosters a deeper connection with God. You learn more about His will for your life as a couple and develop strength to withstand the difficulties that may come. You also discern right from wrong and experience His direction and His correction. Attending church together also plays an integral role in strengthening the marriage relationship. It is widely known that social interactions positively impact your health and well-being by increasing your sense of belonging, boosting your self-confidence, increasing your happiness, and providing emotional support and encouragement during difficult times. Additionally, you get a chance to meet others who share similar interests, and as you form lasting relationships with others, stress is minimized. The positive sense of well-being developed through social interactions serves as a building block for a happy and healthy marriage.

Believing that executing these principles into our married life would produce lasting, positive effects, Mark and I implemented them, and sure enough, we could see the rewards! Everything was going great, the blessings were flowing down, and we continuously gave God the praise. Sometimes as married couples, we can become so wrapped up in our own desires and our accomplishments that we forget the main thing... God. Keeping God at the center of our marriage is key to saving it, for He is the one who gives us the strength to treat each other right, turn away from temptation, and overcome the challenges that marriage brings. We must recognize that the source of our existence is God. Every married couple establishing a family should keep this in mind. He created families. He provides for them and prospers them. He blesses each member with talents. Every blessing that the family receives comes from Him and Him only. If you are in the process of establishing a family and you are reading this book, ask yourself these questions: What kind of family am I building? Is it God-centered or self-centered? If it is not God-centered, it is easier for the devil to wreak havoc in our families and in our lives. He seeks to destroy families by subtly introducing envy, dishonesty, infidelity, and doubt into relationships. He promotes self-love as a virtue and makes it appear more desirable than love for God and love for each other. He creates conflicts between husband and wife, and stirs up rebellion in children, and as the family falls apart, he sits back and laughs. Why? Because he understands that the family is the backbone of the church and the society, so to destroy both he launches his attacks on the family.

Five

FALLING SHORT OF THE IDEAL

GROWING UP, I ALWAYS dreamt of having a family of my own. However, my dream stretched way beyond that. I wanted the perfect family. From early childhood, families like the Huxtables, the Bradys, and the Waltons influenced my thought process and created a vivid and sometimes unrealistic picture of the ideal family. I wanted a family where love reigned supreme, a family in which there were no disagreements, no fussing, and no fighting. I wanted to marry my knight in shining armor, be compatible with him, and together raise beautiful and successful children. I wanted us to be successful enough to own our own home, but most importantly, I wanted a relationship based on friendship, commitment, and continuous romance.

I yearned for something a little different from and a little better than the home in which I was raised. Growing up, I constantly heard my mom accusing my father of infidelity. She was constantly fussing and crying about his alleged affairs, and he was constantly denying every accusation she threw his way. As a teen, I found myself in the middle of their tumultuous relationship, and I dreaded every thought that my father would bring such hurt to my mom whom I loved so much. They were never outwardly affectionate to each other, or should I say, I never was privy to it. I never saw him hug and kiss her. I never saw him slap her behind as she walked past him. Mr. Huxtable did it! As a child growing up, I was never blessed to see the positive aspects of their relationship because my little mind only absorbed the negative. Parents must be careful of their behaviors in front of their children because their actions can lead to adverse childhood experiences, experiences that children may never recover from. I am sure that my mom and dad may have had a positive side to their relationship, but in my little mind, the positivity was clouded by the tumultuous side that I saw. As I observed the hurt my mom was experiencing, I secretly began to dislike my dad because I did not like the pain and the hurt my mom was going through.

My father had a good job with a reputable company, but on evenings and weekends he did a second job as a taxi driver to make extra money. I remember occasions when he would be restlessly looking through the drapes, and my mom would suggest to me that he was looking through the window to see when his "lady" would walk down the street. Not long after, the alleged perpetrator would walk down the street, and amid an erupting word battle between my mom and my dad, my dad would leave to go and drive his taxi. I remember an occasion when my mom followed him, ran down the steps, and hopped into the passenger side of the vehicle. They began yelling at each other. She finally exited the vehicle and returned to the house with tears streaming down her face. My mom was constantly sad and depressed over his alleged affairs. I hated being a part of their mess. I wished it would all go away, but it lingered for as long as I could remember.

On another occasion, my mom and I were in the town waiting for transportation to go home when we spotted the alleged perpetrator. My mom decided that we would wait clandestinely until my father drove up to the taxi stand. Cars came, filled up and left, and we waited. We waited, and she waited. My mom insisted that the alleged perpetrator was hanging around waiting on my dad. We managed to remain discreet, and as my father's car drove up, and the woman tried to open the passenger front door, my mom pushed herself into the front seat and slammed the door. In shock, the woman walked away. I hopped into the back seat, and two passengers came in beside me. With this drama unfolding in front of a waiting crowd, my father must have been embarrassed, but he remained quiet. As a child, I was privy to all this drama taking place in my family. After these childhood experiences, I knew I wanted a family that was different. I wanted a perfect family, a home in which love, peace, and happiness resided. There was no way Mark and I would have that fussing and fighting, that infidelity and insecurity. No way! We were the perfect couple, and we vowed to build the perfect family, or so I thought!

Amid the glow in our eyes, the doting over each other, the unshakable sense of bliss, a huge problem was creeping in! Mark was still not gainfully employed. Being new to the area, he would have to work at increasing his clientele, so the hope was that when I went off to work, he would go out looking for clients and establish himself as a new electrician in town. Early in our marriage, he managed to secure a few jobs here and there, and I was happy that he was trying. Now, months into our marriage, I was noticing a trend. He was asleep when I left for work, and when I returned and asked him about his day, his response rarely included that he was out looking for work. He rarely had enough money to help with paying bills, and I became the breadwinner of our home. I take full responsibility for this because I knew about the instability of his job and that he was not financially capable of carrying out his God given responsibility, but I conceded to marry him anyway. It was my hope that when we got married, he would become a little more responsible in finding work. *Things were going to change,* I thought. Mark was too loving and too involved with God to not take care of his family. As time went by, nothing seemed to change, and I began to accept it. I told myself that as long as Mark was in my life, loving me, everything would be okay. I was blinded by love. I did not look beyond the present and thought only about the love, romance, and companionship I was momentarily experiencing. As long as we were together, nothing else mattered. Money paled in his presence. I was infatuated and did not know it.

As time went on, Mark continued to shirk his responsibility, and I continued to let him. I was so bent on creating "the perfect marriage" that I disregarded the problem and barely brought it up. I told myself that the love we shared was too great to be dismantled by such a trivial thing. I allowed myself to be blinded by love, and without realizing it, Mark began to take precedence in my life. He consumed my thoughts, my actions, and my very existence. Though disappointed by his actions, I dismissed the thought because I was in love with the feeling of love. I was more concerned with how Mark made me feel than the repercussions of his actions. Mark's lack of motivation to find work was putting a strain on our marriage, but I pretended it was not happening. I refused to see the problem for what it was because I was more concerned about the emotional gratification Mark brought to my life. Was Mark a selfish guy? I refused to entertain such a thought. He brought me too much love! Yes, Mark may have fallen short of the mark, but I loved him.

Incidentally, I was falling short of the mark, too. I had made a promise to God to make Him the central focus of my life, and I strayed from my commitment. I allowed myself to become too wrapped up in Mark, and the more I spent time with him, the less time I spent with God. We still prayed together as a family, but my personal connection with God was waning. I spent little time in personal devotion and little time in meaningful prayer. Without realizing it, Mark became first place in my life. Sadly, he became the God in my life, and I neglected an important principle, "Thou shall have no other gods before me" (Exodus 20: 3). I found myself doing whatever Mark wanted, and I began to sacrifice my deeply rooted principles and convictions for him. My relationship with Mark took precedence over everything. With him in my life, nothing else mattered.

Sometimes we allow ourselves to be so consumed by the things and people around us that we begin to lose focus. We enter marriage with the determination to do what is right but allow ourselves to become so sidetracked by the many forces clamoring for our attention: our jobs, our spouses, our financial obligations, etc. We must be very careful not to let our relationships, and the demands and distractions of life take precedence over our relationship with God. It is possible as young married couples to fall into this predicament. We become so wrapped up in our marriage and the gratification it brings that we end up having less room in our hearts for God. With less room in our hearts for God, we are more susceptible to making mistakes and falling prey to the darts of the enemy. Yes, Mark and I seemed to have a duo relationship with God, but it soon became routine. What we needed to work on also was a one-on-one connection with God. Married couples who develop a one-on-one connection with God do not sacrifice their deeply rooted principles and convictions to fulfill each other's needs. They think primarily about the consequences of their actions on their relationship with God. They do not follow each other into sin because they personally know God and accept His will for their lives. God's will for their lives take precedence over everything they do.

Mark and I had been living in our apartment for a little over one year when I broke the news to him that I was taking a loan to purchase some land and build us a house.

He thought it was a great idea and was in total harmony with my decision. I designed the layout and found an architect to draw the plan. When he was finished, I was well pleased with the design. We were going to have our own home, and we were excited. A few months after that I had another surprise for Mark. I was pregnant! I was going to have his baby, our baby! We were happy. Our dream of raising a child or children was coming true. I cannot fully express how I felt at that time. Elated is putting it mildly. Did I fully contemplate the financial repercussions of these decisions? No, I did not, for Mark was still not gainfully employed. He was still making little effort to find work. I had become the sole provider of our home, and it did not seem to bother him. After all, what could be better than to lie in bed and have someone take care of you? I told myself that I loved Mark, and I would not allow his lack of financial diligence to bother me, but unconsciously, it did. In my heart, I knew that Mark was falling short of the ideal, and I hated it.

Six

REMOLDING MARK

Construction began. The house was being built within walking distance from our apartment, and I had hoped that Mark would have become actively involved in its construction, but again, he chose the passive role. He made little effort to get involved. He was just there, a not so innocent bystander! Though I was pregnant, I was left with no choice but to take on the leading role in the construction of our new home. I shopped for the materials and oversaw its construction, and when it was finished, it looked beautiful. The house was beautifully designed with bay windows and shingled roof. We were excited to move in and to begin decorating it. Mark could not contribute financially, so again, I was on my own. I bought furniture, decorations, drapes, and all the accessories needed to make it look lavish.

It did not take me long to become dissatisfied with the role I had taken on and dissatisfied with Mark. He was lacking one trait in the mold of "my ideal husband." Don't get me wrong. Mark was still a loving guy. In many ways, he treated me like a queen. He was patient, understanding, and compassionate, and never raised his voice or his hands at me. However, he was missing a key ingredient necessary to fully savor our relationship. I needed a breadwinner, a hardworking man who would work diligently to supply the needs of his family, not one who would lie in bed while his wife went out and did all the hard work. I could have excused Mark's behavior if I came home to a well-kept house, food already prepared, and laundry handled; however, I still had to come home after a hard day's work and attend to the home. I still had to arise early in the morning to prepare meals for Mark and me because he did not know how to cook, and he made no effort to learn. I still returned and found dirty dishes in the sink and still had to clean and wash clothes on weekends. Everything fell back on me. Mark was not allowing me to be his helper. He was making me his slave, and he did not feel guilty about this recourse.

There and then I decided that Mark needed remolding. I spent numerous hours trying to determine ways to help Mark become more productive. There are just some people who need a push, and I thought that Mark was one of them. I knew he had potential, and I wanted him to reach for it. I wanted him to work alongside me because I knew that if we worked together, we could accomplish a lot in our marriage. However, he was not up to the challenge, and I felt cheated. I was left with little choice but to try and transform him into a more productive and worthy husband.

Mark would not go out looking for work, so I set out to find work for him. Despite the financial difficulties, I asked

Mark if he wanted me to take a loan and buy him a car to drive as a taxi. Mark gladly agreed, and I set out to make this happen. Having a taxi would allow Mark to contribute to the finances of the home. I also expected that he would make the monthly car payments. A driver who faithfully works his taxi should make enough money to run a home. This would be a decent start for Mark. What more could a man want? He was not trying to establish himself as a self-employed electrician or trying to find work with an electrical contractor, and I was not prepared to take care of him for the rest of his life. He was not trying to better himself, so I set out to better him. It was not my intention to control Mark or force a change upon him. Neither was it my intention to make him feel inferior in any way. I was simply trying to help him take up a leadership role rather than the passive one he had chosen. I wanted him to be an assertive and responsible man, one who goes out of his way to ensure that his family's needs are met. To me, that was not asking too much from a man who had promised so much.

Mark's lack of diligence baffled me, especially knowing that we had a shared commitment to make each other better. His choice to remain idle instead of trying to find work thwarted this commitment, so it set me to thinking: Was Mark a lazy guy? If he was lazy, then would buying a taxi make a difference? What if he still didn't go out and work? Could I handle the car payment by myself? What if he was narcissistic? Would he understand my act of compassion? Would he appreciate my kindness? These are some of the questions I contemplated, but in my immaturity, I did not seek to find answers. Had I seriously given them some thought, I would have realized that you cannot change someone who is lazy by giving him or her work. The change must come from within. Similarly, if he was narcissistic, he would not appreciate my compassion or even understand it, but instead he would take my kindness for weakness and use it as a weapon against me. The extreme love he had for himself might make him feel so deserving of my compassion and foster feelings of entitlement. I dismissed these thoughts, for after all, Mark was my husband, and I loved him.

Finally, we got the car. At the sight of the car, Mark's mouth fell open and his eyes opened wide. The car was beautiful and expensive-looking. Before he could even say thank you, he began asking for money to beautify the car even further. He wanted broad rims, spacers, stereo, large speakers, and tinted windows. He wanted it all. Not only did Mark want all of these accessories added to the car, but he also wanted them to be done immediately, and they must all be completed before he begins to work the taxi. So bent was I on fulfilling Mark's desires that I began putting myself more and more into debt to supply them. I readily sacrificed my Christian principles for him, and the more I strived to supply his desires, the less I began to focus on God. There were times I even withheld tithes and offerings to meet Mark's needs. I ignored a very important principle that I had previously vowed to live by: "...Thou shalt worship the Lord thy God, and him only shalt thou serve (Matt 4:10).

Finally, Mark began to work his taxi. I was joyful that he would have the finances necessary to support the home.

Ready for his first day at work, he admired the car as it stood in the driveway. It shined like gold. I could sense it was dear to his heart. It was a car every young man would dream to drive. He had the broad rims, the spacers, the music, and the tinted windows. He was elated and ever joyful. He could not believe that the car was his. He waved at me as he left to make his first trip. I was happy for him. Now he could help to support our family. Now he would become the leader of his home. Day after day he would return home and spread out the money he made. A feeling of manliness came over him. I could see it in his eyes, and I was ecstatic. On returning home, he would throw the money up in the air and let it fall to the ground. That was his way of saying, "Look at me. I am rich!" Mark was now helping me with groceries, paying bills, and helping to prepare for the arrival of our son. Just like the potter churns out his clay to create a better design, I felt like Mark was being reshaped into someone more productive and worthwhile. An inexplicable joy overpowered me, and my face regained its healthy glow. Once again, Mark was the ideal man I yearned for, and I was well pleased with his new look.

A few months later, our baby boy arrived. We were elated! He was a great addition to our family. The nursery was fully decorated with a crib and matching chest of drawers. A beautiful blue sheet-set and matching pillows accentuated the space. Blue balloons, a "Welcome Home" sign, and an "It's a Boy" poster welcomed his arrival. Mark was excited to be a dad and was most of all happy to have a son. We enjoyed every moment together as we watched our baby boy transition from newborn to infant to toddler. Mark was thrilled! He had so many plans to get his son involved in sports and to introduce him to the things that he liked doing. You could sense his adoration for his baby boy by the way he sang to him, spun him around, and continuously kissed him.

    Things were going great for our family, and I was so happy. I thought about my mom and how pleased she must be to see the great family I had built. It was no secret to her that I sought a family much better than the one in which I was raised. She knew I wanted better and admired me for it. My dad did not live to see this day, for less than two months after our wedding, he died. Oh, how I wished he were here to see how happy Mark and I were in our marriage. I reflected on the family I had created. What a beautiful design it now was!

Seven

THE TRANSFORMATION

MONTHS PASSED BY AND **Mark** faithfully made payments on the car, bought groceries, and paid bills. He boasted to me about how many friends he was making as he drove his taxi. At that time, he was 27 years old. As a young man driving a fancy car, he began to attract a crowd. The young men were crazy about his car, and it did not take me long to realize that the young ladies were crazy about him, too. Everyone seemed to know him, and he became the most popular young guy in town. Whenever we drove through the town together, young ladies would call out to him giving him seductive and flirtatious looks, and I could not help but notice how uneasy he became. One day while we were driving and stuck in traffic, we were boldly approached by a young lady who pushed her head into his window talking to him in a flirtatious way. She inspected my son and me as she continued her flirtatious discourse. I asked Mark for an explanation, but he had nothing substantial to give. He claimed that she was just a passenger who previously traveled with him. Similar events started occurring, and each time they took place, I noticed that he would never introduce me as his wife. When I raised the issue in conversation, he would say that I was just a jealous wife, and they were all friends he made while driving his taxi.

As time went by, I could sense a change in Mark's demeanor. He became very reclusive. The money wasn't going up in the air anymore; neither was any coming down. He was returning to his old self and had little money to contribute to groceries and bills. He began to make lots of excuses. The excuses ranged from having a flat tire, to the check engine light coming on, to the engine leaking oil. He always had something to fix. He seemed to be a regular visitor to the mechanic shop but could never produce any evidence of his claims. The car I bought was in good mechanical condition, and the strange thing was that it never broke down on weekends when we drove together as a family. After six consecutive months of making car payments, Mark was coming up short of his payments and started asking if I could help. Not for the life of me could I understand Mark's drastic change. He had promised me that he would pay for the car, yet he became so delinquent with his payments that the bank started automatic deductions from my account. This was disastrous. Now I would have to pay for the car, pay for the house, buy groceries, pay utilities, pay the babysitter, and take care of my child all by myself if Mark made a complete regression back to his old self.

This trend continued for months. I became more and more unhappy, and Mark became more and more distant.

As was customary, Mark would leave early every morning to make a few trips before returning to take our baby to the babysitter and take me to the bus station. From the bus station, I would take a bus into the city where I worked. Oftentimes I waited and waited, and Mark never showed. On some occasions, I was forced to walk with our baby in my arms all the way to the babysitter and then to the bus station because it was getting late. Mark did not seem to care for me anymore. Within a matter of months, my joy had turned to sadness, and I began to feel depressed. On my way back from work, I would stop and wait on the main road for Mark to pick me up and take me to the babysitter to get our son. Oftentimes, it would be a long time before he arrived. At least if Mark had no regard for my time, I wished he would have shown some regard for the babysitter's time. I could sense her annoyance whenever I arrived late because she was being forced to work beyond her scheduled hours, and I did not have extra money to compensate her accordingly.

One day while I was waiting and waiting, Mark drove up and in the back seat was a young lady holding our son.

"It was getting late, so I went ahead and picked him up," Mark explained.

"I have been waiting here for two hours," I said in a disgusted tone. I gave him a look as to demand to know who was holding my child. He turned around and said,

"Oh, this is a friend. Her Name is Abbie. She was the only remaining passenger, and she didn't mind waiting in the car until I picked him up," he said.

Mark dropped off the baby and me at the house and left with the young lady to continue making his trips. I was highly aggravated and felt insulted. I did not want to jump to conclusions, but something seemed wrong with that picture. I didn't want to believe that Mark was having an affair because he still portrayed a sense of spirituality. He still read the Bible and was still fascinated with spiritual ideologies. He was heavily involved in church and was now the lead Bible instructor. I told myself that I was doubtful because I was just a jealous wife. After all, I had heard this term so often from Mark that I started to believe it. I also wanted to believe Mark when he said that the devil was putting doubts in my head to cause a breakup of our marriage. He assured me that no one would ever come between us. Each time Mark realized I was on to something, he would become a little more caring and a little more concerned, yet, despite his reassurance, I sensed that something was up. He was coming home later and later. I felt like we were growing apart, and whenever I tried to talk to him about our relationship, he would say that nothing was wrong with our relationship, and I was only imagining things.

I didn't want to believe that after three years of courtship and three years of marriage, my life would take such a downward turn. Mark and I became total strangers. He continued to stay out late and sometimes stayed out the entire night. My sleep pattern was interrupted because when he was out, it was very difficult for me to fall asleep. I would lie in bed and allow my thoughts to wander. My thoughts wandered aimlessly in search of answers to the many questions that now troubled my soul. Why was Mark coming home so late? Was he out working as he claimed, or was he having an affair?

Mark became very secretive and full of lies. He began to hide things from me, and each discovery, he covered up with an impromptu lie. I found condoms hidden under the car seat and started seeing stains on his underwear and marks on his chest. Each time that I confronted him, he had a ready excuse. He claimed that we must have bought the car with the condoms already there. He never could explain the state of the underwear but brushed it off as old stains. As for the marks on his chest, chemicals sometimes splashed on his chest whenever he was cleaning the car. He kept a straight face as he poured out lie upon lie. He must have thought me to be foolhardy, for some of the lies were so absurd. Little did Mark know; I was no fool! There is an old saying from my childhood that suggests if you want to catch a vulture, you should pretend to be dead. Thinking that you are a dead body, the vulture will descend upon you, and then you can grab him. The saying suggests that you can pretend to be ignorant to catch someone in the act. In my sadness, I decided to play along, but all the while, I was hoping to be wrong. I still desperately loved Mark.

As I reflected on my life and my marriage, I became very depressed and anxious, and each day, I lazed around the house feeling sorry for myself. I began to lose interest in everything around me, and with each passing day, I became more and more tearful. I felt alone. I felt empty. I did not know where to turn. How could this happen to me? This was not the life I bargained for. How did I fall victim to such unhappiness? I felt like a kite giving way to the restless wind. I was going down, down, down. My life was about to crumble. I found myself living with a total stranger. I could not help but notice the subtle transformation, the metamorphosis. As a caterpillar transforms itself into a butterfly, so did my husband's character transform before my eyes. This could not be the man I married. His transformation completely baffled me. Now he was a different person. An imposter now lived in my home, ate at my table, and slept in my bed.

Eight

REVELATIONS OF INFIDELITY

THOUGH ROCKY, I FOUGHT desperately to hold my marriage together, but it seemed like I was fighting the battle alone. At the onset of our relationship, we had made a promise to weave our lives together, hold on to each other, and not let go no matter what was thrown in our direction, but it seemed as though Mark had forgotten that promise. The closeness we shared was slowly diminishing, and I felt disconnected from him. He was constantly out of the house, we were hardly spending quality time together, and the once unshakable sense of bliss had now turned into constant fussing. I felt hurt and let down by Mark, but the hurt I was experiencing did not seem to faze him. He continued to deny that anything was going wrong in our marriage and insisted that it was all in my imagination.

One late evening, Mark brought two passengers to our home to introduce them to me. It did not take me long to recognize that one of them was the young lady who was previously holding my son. I remained calm as he introduced them.

"This is Abbie, and this is Joy," he said. "I'll be studying the Bible with them. They're really excited to learn!"

"Nice to meet you all," I exclaimed. I acted as though I had never met Abbie before. I'm sure Mark thought that I didn't remember her. It turned out that the two girls were best friends and were regular passengers in his taxi. He introduced them to me as his friends. His two friends were 18 years old, so I chose to make nothing of it. They sat in the living room, and as they looked around, I began conversing with them. They were seated right next to a stack of photo albums, so I handed the stack to them.

"You can look through these if you'd like," I said.

Joy took the stack and handed one to Abbie. Joy then randomly picked the wedding album. She looked through and asked us questions about the pictures. When she was through, she tried to hand it over to Abbie, who quickly pushed it away. Joy looked to see if I noticed, so I looked the other way. They then cunningly looked at each other. Abbie looked through all the other albums, but the wedding album she refused to touch. This behavior made me a bit suspicious, and in my mind, I began to question Mark's relationship with her.

As time went by, the signs kept showing up. Mark continued to come home in the wee hours of the morning with little money to show for his late work and subtle evidence of infidelity kept popping up. Each time that they popped up, Mark dismissed them as untrue. It was at this challenging point in our relationship that our picture that had hung majestically in the same spot, untouched, in our living room for about three years as a symbol of our devotion and love, suddenly fell to the ground and shattered into pieces. Deep within my heart, I wondered if the broken picture was a sign that Mark had broken our marriage vows. I hated the thought of what the answer could be. The more I thought about my situation, the more I became depressed. Mark continued to be very distant, and I continued to be very confused. Not for the life of me could I fathom his transformation. We continued to attend church on weekends with the pretense that everything was okay. One afternoon after church, a visitor who visited occasionally to play the piano pulled me to the side.

"I believe that your husband is up to no good," he said. "What time did he come home last night?" I was speechless and very nervous.

"Late. About 1:00 AM," I responded.

"I think he is seeing someone who lives close to me. His car is always parked up by her house. He was there up to late last night." There was a period of silence between us. I did not know what to say. I kept my gaze to the floor. When I looked up, my watery eyes met his empathetic stare. He placed a comforting arm around me and said, "You do not deserve this!" With that he walked away.

I left church that day with a feeling of heaviness in my heart. I should have been glad to know the truth, but I was not, for the truth was too painful.

"Oh Lord," I cried. "When will my troubles be over?"

Church was the one place I found comfort and peace, and now the troubles had followed me into the pew. This was the place I could lay my burdens down and trust that He would sustain me. This was my safe haven! Now I would have to worry about who would give me discomforting news when I walk through the church door. I knew he meant well, but I felt he should have waited rather than give me the discomforting news at church. My world was crumbling. Everywhere I went trouble was right at my heel.

One morning, I waited for Mark to return home to give me a ride into town. It became very late, and Mark did not show up. I was very tired and dreaded having to walk all the way into town to catch the bus to get to work. Mark had promised to return and take me to the bus station, and now if I waited any longer, it would be too late for me to get to work on time. I could no longer rely on Mark to keep his word. I was now almost two months pregnant with our second child, and he did not seem to care. I left the house and began the dreaded walk into town. The morning sickness was kicking in making every step a struggle. I felt bloated and nauseous. Luckily, a taxi driver came down the street to drop off a passenger. He must have been heaven-sent. I got into the front seat and breathed a sigh of relief. I was the only passenger in the car, and as he was driving, I felt a sense of uneasiness coming from him. Finally, he broke the silence as he said,

"You are married to a real street boy!"

"What do you mean?" I asked nervously.

"Here you are, going to work every day, and as soon as you leave to go to work, he brings his woman friend into your house." I was dumbfounded. My heart began to race. "I work around here every day. I see what he's doing. Are you both married?" he asked.

"Yes," I responded.

In a very disgusted voice, he blurted out what seemed to be a rhetorical question. "What kind of man brings his affair partner into his house that he shares with his wife?" After a moment of silence, he answered the question himself. "Only a bum!"

I was at a loss for words. The driver probably wondered why I wasn't saying anything. I was hurt. I got out of the taxi and boarded a bus for work. I laid my head back on the bus headrest and reflected on what the driver had said. A feeling of sadness came over me. I felt defeated. *How could Mark change so much?* I thought to myself. *Here I am, pregnant with his baby, and he doesn't even care if I collapse in the heat of the day walking to catch a taxi to go to work. Here I am struggling to pay the bills while he is enjoying himself at the house.* I was hurt.

I approached Mark that night with what I had heard, and he became very defensive and angry. "Show me the driver who said those lying words to you," he demanded. "He must be jealous of us!"

"Why would he make all this up?" I asked. "He doesn't even know me. He has nothing to gain by making this up."

"People hate to see good things and would try their best to destroy other people's relationships when theirs aren't going good," Mark retorted.

I wanted to believe Mark. Maybe the driver did want to break up our marriage. Maybe he was jealous of Mark and his relationship with me. Maybe he was jealous of the beautiful home we built and the fancy car Mark drove. These were all Mark's words, and even though I believed that the man was telling the truth, Mark was so skilled in manipulating my mind and causing me to doubt myself and the obvious truth before me that I unconsciously gave in to his tactics. In fact, I started feeling sorry for him. I hated that people would plot to destroy him and our marriage. I began to feel animosity toward the driver, just like he made me feel animosity toward the visiting pianist at church. Mark was a master in eliciting my compassion and sorrow, and in the end, he always won. I always gave in to him and his desires. The hurtful thing about the whole situation was— I still loved Mark.

One Sunday, I was home alone and feeling very down. I lazed around the house doing housework and tried to lift my mood by listening to music. My baby boy was at my mom's, and Mark was out working his taxi. After finishing my housework, I sluggishly laid on the sofa and fell fast asleep. Every day I felt lethargic and unmotivated. I no longer had interest in the activities I once enjoyed. I did not go to the mall, and I no longer wanted to be a part of social gatherings. Mark and I rarely attended sporting activities. I went to work because I had no choice and because I needed the money to pay the bills. I did not cease to attend church, for it was there I sought comfort and strength to carry on.

I got up from the sofa and mustered up the courage to catch some sunlight. I opened the door and stepped outside, and as I stood outside, the fresh air comfortingly embraced me. I looked up to the sky and began to pray. "I am confused," I said to God. "I need answers," I continued. "I have so many unanswered questions... Please help me!" A host of unanswered questions was tearing my soul apart. I wanted to believe all Mark's excuses so that I would save myself the pain, the sorrow, and the heartbreak. I knew God had promised to not give us more than we could bear, but somehow, the burden was just too heavy for me. The sunlight rested on the bushes that grew at the side of the house. The birds sang a joyful tune. Grasshoppers danced from leaf to leaf. Butterflies enjoyed nature and God's handiwork. Every creature around me was happy, except me.

Suddenly my eyes glanced into a patch of bushes. A heap of torn up paper caught my attention. On one of the pieces, I saw the word, "Karen." I looked at the paper again and read the word, "Karen." *Who could be writing about me?* I questioned myself. I could tell it was a letter that was ripped up. I bent myself into the bushes and collected each piece of torn up paper. I was curious to know its contents. I ran back to the house with a determination to piece them together and read every word. Like a jigsaw puzzle, I put it all together and fastened it with tape. I gazed at my finished product. It did not take me long to realize that the letter was written to my husband. I looked to the end of the letter which read,

"Love Abbie." I had heard the name before. In fact, I had met her before. She was the young lady holding my son that day. She was the young lady who visited my home with her friend Joy. I became more and more curious.

As I began to read the letter, my jaw dropped. With every line I read, the tears began to flow. The words that I read were devastating. I read the letter a second time for fear I was hallucinating, but no, I was not! By the time I was through, I was sobbing loudly. I began to shake. I held in my hands evidence of infidelity. I was hurt beyond measure. I felt as though someone had taken a dagger and pierced it through my heart. How could my husband whom I loved so dearly perform such a wicked act? In the letter, Abbie wrote about their wonderful night together. She wrote about his plans to build them a house so they could be together forever. She also wrote about missing her monthly cycle and how scared she was. "Oh God in heaven help me!" I cried. My head was about to explode and shatter into pieces. I felt betrayed. I cried, and I cried. I could not believe my eyes.

Nine

THE CONFRONTATION

NIGHT CAME, AND I tried to fall asleep. The roosters were lying soundly. The dogs had ceased their barking, yet no matter how hard I tried, I could not fall asleep. Mark was still out. I waited patiently for him to come home. It was 1:00 AM when I heard the car pull up in the driveway. I approached Mark about the letter the minute he walked in. Again, he had excuses. Someone was trying to set him up. He was positive that someone wrote that letter, ripped it up, and threw it there to make it look like it was his.

"So, they came all the way down to our house in this cul-de-sac and threw it there?" I asked.

"Of course, because I have no idea where that letter came from or who wrote it," he replied. "People will go to every length to break up a marriage! This is all a hoax. I will surely catch the culprit," he continued.

"So, they're lying about your night with her and about her missing her menstrual cycle? I continued.

"Of course! Abbie has a boyfriend. That has nothing to do with me!" With that, he threw himself in the bed.

I could not believe how much Mark had grown into a liar. Deep down inside, I knew that Mark was not telling the truth, yet to soften the pain I was feeling, I accepted it. By thwarting my emotions, I allowed an emotional volcano to build up in my head, creating psychological distress and symptoms. I was constantly exhausted and unable to concentrate. Self-defeating and self-damaging thoughts began to infiltrate my mind, and I became very irrational to the point that I almost put my life at risk. One night as my son lay asleep in the crib, I decided to go in search of Mark. I was at my wits' end and could not take it anymore. I decided to go to the main road, wait for him, and confront him to see what he was doing. To the left of my house was a wide gravel track, a shortcut to the main road. Thick, heavy bushes lined the track, and there were no streetlights along the way. I had never walked that way in the dark, yet I took that way that night. I remember thinking that I would not even mind if someone just jumped out of the bushes and ended my life. I was overwhelmed and did not feel I could go on. It was almost midnight when I left. I found myself alone on the main road. I stood there in tears. A short time after, I heard loud music coming down the street. It was the only car in sight. I recognized the car to be Mark's. Suddenly, a distance away from me, the car halted. Mark hurried out and asked me what I was doing there. He seemed very nervous, and he motioned to his friend Rex to drive the car away. Rex hurried to the driver seat and quickly sped away. I never got to see who was in the car with them, but my imagination began to run wild.

"Why did you come out here this late?" he asked. "Are you losing your mind?"

"I have had enough of this," I responded. "I am not putting up with this anymore!" The truth of the matter was, I was losing my mind. I was allowing myself to be hurt so much that I was losing my ability to reason and make sound judgement calls. I was being made to feel so worthless that I no longer valued my life. By fostering all the hurt, disappointment, and discouragement in my life, I had let go of myself emotionally, physically, and spiritually. My sense of well-being deteriorated, and my life lost vitality, meaning, and purpose. Frankly, I had lost the zeal to live.

"I have to walk out to the main road to get the car and take Rex home. I will be back soon," Mark said. My heart was aching. I knew within my heart that Abbie was in that car. I knew that Rex drove off in an effort to conceal the truth. I stood in silence as Mark walked out the door. My heart sunk. I felt rejected and unloved. I lay in the bed and cried myself to sleep. It would be hours before Mark returned.

A few weeks later, I was sitting at my job, when the receptionist called for me. Someone by the name of Joy was at the reception desk wanting to see me.

Joy, who's joy? I wondered. I boarded the elevator, made my way down to the lobby, and saw Abbie's friend waiting there. I recognized her the moment I saw her. She had come to my house that day with Abbie.

"Do you have a moment? I would like to speak to you," she uttered.

Uneasy, I said, "Okay." Joy had an earful for me. She came to reveal to me the truth about Mark and Abbie. Abbie was Mark's girlfriend. Joy and Rex were boyfriend and girlfriend, and the four of them often double-dated. Rex had been to my home many times before. He spent a lot of time with Mark. He sometimes rode along with Mark when Mark was working late; however, before that night when he speedily drove off the car, I never imagined that he would be a co participant in such deception. Joy told it all! She revealed that Mark hardly worked his taxi, and the four of them spent most of the time hanging out together in all types of secluded places. She claimed that she considered herself an accomplice to a very wicked act and had come to apologize.

Hurt, I blurted out, "Why are you just now telling me this? Didn't you have enough time to tell me this? Why now?"

I felt crushed, but determined not to show my defeat, I turned everything back on Joy. "Maybe you wanted him, too, and couldn't get him, so you're upset!"

Joy had an inexplicable look of sadness in her eyes. She stood to her feet and stared at my fragile and helpless body. As if in disbelief, she uttered, "You are such a fool! He has you really fooled."

She quickly made her way out of the building. I tried to conceal my shaking. I made my way into the elevator and up to the office where I worked. I sat at my desk grieving. I tried to concentrate on my work but could not clear my mind. I was hurting. How could Mark do this to me? Was

Joy speaking the truth? Was she just trying to destroy my marriage? Mark had trained me to believe that everyone was against our relationship. In the depths of my mind, he stored the thought that assailants aspired to break us up. I wrestled with the thoughts that consumed me. I didn't know what to believe. I tried desperately hard to do my job, but I could not. I felt cold inside. I was shaking.

I went to my supervisor to let him know that I was not feeling well. He agreed that I could leave. I quickly made my way out of the building. In the blazing heat of the day, the coldness lingered. I continued to shake. I made my way to the taxi stand and boarded a waiting taxi. It all seemed like a dream. I arrived at the town in an instant. Outside my subdivision was a waiting taxi. It was empty. Normally drivers would remain for a while to accumulate a full load of passengers. I boarded the waiting taxi, and the driver immediately sped away. In an instant, I was at my front door. I unlocked the door and heard footsteps running. I looked around the hallway and glimpsed my husband hurrying back to our room. I made a quick trail behind him and found myself at his heels. I began screaming for fear of what I might confront. Mark plunged himself into the room and tried to close the door. I tried desperately to keep the door open, and he tried desperately to shut me out.

"I'm begging you, Karen, do not come in!" he yelled.

My left hand was being crushed in the doorway. "Open the door," I yelled, and I pushed more and more. Mark continued to petition that I stay out of the room.

"I am begging you," he yelled again, "do not come in!"

He was determined to keep me out, so he continued pushing the door. I was yelling, and I was shaking. I was cold sweating, and my heart was racing. I continued to scream even more. He continued to beg me to stay out. In the room, I could hear movements and someone whispering. I could tell Mark was buying time, maybe allowing the person to get dressed. I kept my hands in the doorway to deter him from completely shutting me out. Suddenly, I heard the bedroom window opening. I let go of the door, ran to the kitchen, and grabbed the biggest knife. I made my way out the door and around the house to the back. I arrived in time to see Abbie jumping through my bedroom window. I quickly built up speed and was right upon her when she turned the corner. As I tried to turn the corner, I skidded and slammed into a concrete fence post. I fell to the ground, my head spinning. I got up and proceeded after her. With the knife still in my hand, I made my way after her. I looked back and saw Mark coming. Mark grabbed me and began dragging me back to the house. I fought back, but he overpowered me.

"You're embarrassing me!" he yelled. "Get back into the house!" He continued pulling me home. "This young lady is pregnant, and you made her have to jump through the window."

Mark was fuming. He pulled me straight to the house. I went inside, threw myself on the floor, and cried. I got up and repeatedly banged my head and my body against the wall. I was losing my mind and did not care that I was pregnant. I hated life. I hated my life, and I did not wish to go on. My tears cascaded down like a waterfall. My dream had turned into a nightmare, and I was going berserk. I knew in my heart that my marriage to Mark was over. I screamed, and I screamed, and I screamed. I could not restrain myself. Mark remained on the porch outside. He was probably wondering about Abbie or was either too afraid or too embarrassed to face me. Finally, he came into the room to address me:

"It's not what you're thinking," he said. "She just came to visit me and needed to use the bathroom." After a moment of silence, he continued, "I got scared when I saw you coming, and that's why I acted like that. I knew you were going to overreact, and I reacted out of fear." Mark knew he was lying but continued anyway. "Nothing is going on between us. She's pregnant with her boyfriend's baby. She's just my friend."

He sat on the floor next to me, placed his arms around me, and tried to comfort me. I knocked his hands over and moved away from him. After a long while, I mustered the courage to walk to my bedroom. I stared at the bed and the bed sorrowfully stared back at me. My bed, my sacred bed, was now defiled. That was the bed on which we consummated our marriage. That bed was to be a symbol of purity, commitment, and our eternal love for each other. As I stared at the unmade bed, I could not help but cry. I walked to the open window, raised my fist to the sky and blurted out to God in anger:

"How dare you do this to me! How dare you allow this to happen! Where are you when I need you?"

I was mad with God. I felt let down by Him. There was no way I deserved this! He had promised to protect me from all hardships, and He did not keep His word. *"Why God, why?"* was the grief-stricken cry of my soul. *How could you allow this to happen to me? In fact, how dare you allow this to happen to me!* In my mind, I was the last person deserving of this. As I mentioned previously: Growing up, I thought myself destined for a perfect life— a life filled with joy and happiness. Believing myself to be a good person, I felt sure I should have been handed a pass from trials, tribulations, and pain. I saw myself as gentle, kind, affectionate, and thoughtful. These attributes I thought would guarantee me a life of eternal bliss. Instead, I was handed the gift of woe!

I felt empty, rejected, and forlorn. I had trusted Mark to do what was right for me and the family we committed to raise together, but Mark had betrayed my trust. The hurt was overwhelming. My dream of having the perfect family and a good life was shattered.

Ten

THE SEPARATION

NIGHT CAME, AND MARK believed he once again had me hoodwinked. He was so used to me accepting his behavior and believing his many lies. By now, he was probably confident that he could do anything to me, and I would readily forgive him. I take full responsibility for his misconception because I had allowed him to hurt me repeatedly and without any consequence fall right back into my arms. This time I would prove him wrong. There was no way I could forgive him for his grievous behavior. I kept a low profile and recoiled to the other bedroom. There I could determine my subsequent move.

I lay on the bed and took an introspective look into my sad state of affairs. I tried to find answers to the many difficult questions that plagued my mind. I had none. I was young, angry, and full of hurt. I was not yet ready to be truthful. I wished I knew then what I know now. I was not totally blameless. Although I believed He was, God was not the center of my life. Mark was. Mark had become my God.

I lived for him, and I had begun to remorselessly sacrifice my basic principles for him. I had my view of the perfect marriage, and I tossed God to the side to create my own perfect picture. Was I doing it because it was the right thing to do, or was I doing it to make myself look good? Was I creating a spectacle for others to admire? These were some of the questions I should have answered— truthfully answered! Whether it was for the onlookers or to make myself look good, by going into unnecessary debt, I created unnecessary stress in my marriage that may have helped to send it downhill. I had become overwhelmed with stress, and the more I became overwhelmed with stress, the less I prayed to God and the less I read His word. I found myself going further and further away from Him. My heart was with Mark and the problems that so relentlessly engulfed me. What I thought I was, and what I thought I deserved, I came to realize, I was far from it and totally undeserving of it.

The corn tree stands tall and strong and with pride he declares, "What a strong tree I am!" Suddenly the wind blows, and he finds himself on the ground. He looks up, and in shock he exclaims, "How on earth did I get here?"

A voice resounds in the wind, "Your roots did not go down deep enough."

I used to think I was such a strong Christian, and when my test came, I failed. I used to think that there was no young person more worthy of His bountiful blessings than I. I was wrong. I was so unworthy! No one is worthy! All that He does for us comes from the goodness of His heart. I am sure He wanted to bless me, but I blocked His blessing! I did not afford Him time to bless me in His way and in His time.

Sometimes God's plan and our plans do not mirror each other, and that was the source of my disappointment. I tried to transform Mark instead of allowing God to do His job. I should have let Mark come to his own realization that he needed to fulfill his leadership role, but instead, I enabled him. I became his crutch. I was there to supply his every need, and even when I realized that his behavior was becoming destructive to our marriage, I constantly rescued him from the pitfalls of his destructive trajectory. I took more responsibility for his actions and inaction than he was taking for himself. In my effort to help Mark, I ended up hurting him. Mark did not care to pay for the car, so I paid for it because I did not want to lose it. He did not care to pay the bills, so I paid them all because we needed somewhere to stay. I never allowed him to face the financial consequences of his actions, so he continued his destructive behavior knowing that his devoted wife would always come through for him. Had I not enabled him, he would have eventually gotten up and found work. Had I not become his crutch, he would have learned to provide. He would have learned to be responsible and to take care of his home. By taking over his role, I fostered an infidel. "But if any provide not for his own, and specially for those of his own house, he hath denied the faith, and is worse than an infidel" (1Tim 5:8).

Additionally, I tried to make Mark love me. I tried to buy his love. I should have known that you cannot make someone love you. The fact of the matter is, you can choose who to love, but you cannot choose who will love you back. You can choose who to give your heart to, but you cannot make them give their heart to you. You can shower material gifts upon them, you can supply their every need, but in the end, it is still their choice to love you. Love does not come with a price. You ought to be loved for who you are, not for what you have or what you can give. You can love someone with all your heart, but if they choose not to return that love, it does not mean that something is wrong with you. If you are going through similar experiences, I urge you to lift your head up high and find your strength and happiness in God. Remember, man may fail you, but God never will! You can pick up the pieces and move on with your life.

The time had come for me to decide. I wanted my decision to be purposeful and well thought out. The time had come for me to confront my troubles and not sweep them under the rug as I so often did. I had to make an important decision, and I needed to make it by the morning. I continued to search for answers to the difficult questions that plagued my mind. I tried to figure out whether or not Mark was this way when we got married. Could he have hid himself so well? How could I have missed the signs? I chose to believe that Mark had experienced a culture shock as he ventured into the world of taxi-driving and could not handle it. In an instant, Mark had become the popular guy in town. Prior to our marriage, he had not experienced this type of popularity. He was a simple guy from a simple town who chose a simple conservative life at the tender age of 17. People were drawn to him at church, but that was different. He was never in the fast lane, but this all changed in an instant when he stepped out as a young taxi driver with a fancy, expensive-looking car. Suddenly he was the most important man around town and fell for the fleeting gratification his popularity emitted.

When Mark first began to drive his taxi, he used to tell me everything. I remember him talking and laughing about all the young men wanting to be his friend. He thought it funny that prior to driving the car, no one noticed him. He would laugh and joke about his newfound fame, and he did not hesitate to tell me about his encounters. One young man told him that if the car were his, he would be with all the young ladies in the town. Mark thought that was hilarious. The young man even offered him a bag of condoms, which Mark brought home and gently sat on our dresser promising that he was not about that life. Unfortunately, it was not long before his newfound fame inflated his ego and led to his marital demise. Mark unwittingly fell victim to the trap set for him, and the interest of his newfound friends, he mistook for love. Mark was blindsided and failed to see through the web that the enemy had weaved for him.

I awoke in the morning and asked Mark to pack his things and leave. There was no way I could forgive this grievous act, even if I tried. My son now stayed with my mom during the week, so I was glad he would not be privy to this difficult move. Mark begged me to let him stay, but I stood firm. I was almost sure he felt I would retreat in my decision to let him go. He slowly packed his clothes as if waiting for me to change my mind, but I did not change my mind. The pain I was feeling was unlike any other pain I had felt before. I was in emotional and physical pain. I felt sad, exhausted, and weak. I had no appetite. My heart was skipping beats, and I felt nervous inside. Not only was I cold sweating, but I felt my entire body cramping. It hurt me to know that my unborn baby lay amid this anguish. Mark packed his things and left. As he walked up the street, neighboring dogs barked joyously to his long-awaited sendoff. Every bark was painful, but I had to send him away. I could not allow myself to settle for a life of hurt, pain, and rejection, for I was worth much more than that. I trusted that I could walk this road alone. I was not going to let this crisis bring me down.

Oftentimes when things like this happen, our self-esteem is shattered, and we walk with our head down low. We try to figure out if the infidelity happened because something was wrong with us. I had to convince myself that nothing was wrong with me; instead, Mark cheated because something was wrong with him. He made the choice to have an affair, not because I was not a good wife, but because he was allowed too much power in our relationship, and absolute power corrupts. The power Mark brandished was a very unhealthy power. He asserted a power that was manipulative, unreasonable, and undermining, and I allowed him. As I sought desperately to filter the thoughts that were dragging me down, I reminded myself that I was special, special in the eyes of God. I had to pull myself together and be strong for my son, my unborn baby, and me.

While we do not always have a choice over what happens to us, we always have a choice regarding how we face it. "I will bounce back," I comforted myself. From time to time, I might regress into grief, but I had to refrain from thinking that it all happened to me because God did not love me. There is nothing more important to Him than for me to be happy and fulfilled. When bad things happen to us, He feels our pain, is very present with us, and works to bring out the best in our bad situations. He takes the long view, sees the big picture, and looks to our eternal welfare. Sometimes He does not intervene in our adverse situations or spare us from the consequences of our actions because He desires to teach us a valuable lesson or create an even greater testimony. I am now aware that I was not guaranteed a painless, stress free life, but I am pleased to know that He has promised to hold my hand and walk with me every step of the way.

What God Hath Promised

God hath not promised skies always blue,
Flower-strewn pathways all our lives through;
God hath not promised sun without rain,
Joy without sorrow, peace without pain.
God hath not promised we shall not know
Toil and temptation, trouble and woe;
He hath not told us we shall not bear
many a burden, many a care.
God hath not promised smooth roads and wide,
Swift, easy travel, needing no guide;
Never a mountain rocky and steep,
Never a river turbid and deep
But God hath promised strength for the day,
Rest for the labor, light for the way,
Grace for the trials, help from above,
Unfailing sympathy, undying love

—Annie Johnson Flint

Eleven

IN CLANDESTINE PLACES

WITH MARK GONE, I looked forward to using the time to heal. He moved back in with his parents many miles away. I continued to leave my son at my mom's during the week and bring him home on weekends. He was about one and a half years old when our separation took place. In his little mind, he must have sensed that something was wrong, but amid my sadness, I tried my best to make him happy. He brought life to my weekends, but when he was gone during the week, I endured a rollercoaster of emotions. One day I would be getting over the hurt, then another day it would come right back to me.

One day, I was in a bus coming from work into the town where I lived. Suddenly, I spotted someone who looked like Mark. As I got off the bus, I concealed myself in the distance to take a better look. Sure enough, it was Mark. He stood right opposite a vocational school that I knew Abbie attended. I stood my ground to see what he was doing. Soon Abbie came out of the building, greeted him, and together they walked down the street. Tears came into my eyes as I watched them disappear into the sunlight. The hurt was overwhelming. I was carrying Mark's baby, and that made the pain more excruciating. I walked up the street as I prayed to God to give me the strength to face this difficult time.

Night came, and I tried to fall asleep. About 10:00 PM I heard a knock on the door. I looked out and saw Mark.

"Why are you here?" I asked.

"I came to see my son," he replied. "I miss him. May you open the door?"

"No," I replied. "You are not going to come up here, hang out with your girlfriend, and then use my house as a rest stop! Go back to where you came from!"

"What are you talking about?" he exclaimed. "I don't even know when was the last time I saw Abbie. We don't even talk anymore! I came up here to see you and my son. Please open the door."

Mark was such a liar! I had just seen him with Abbie. "He's not here!" I replied, and with that I closed the drape.

Mark left, and through the window, I could see him stroll up the street. I felt sorry to turn him away because his parents lived a long way from us, but I was determined to make it clear that I was no longer his fool. I would not allow him to keep popping up into my life whenever it was convenient to him. That was wrong, and it was unfair. Mark came around occasionally, not because he cared but because he probably was not allowed to sleep at Abbie's house and did not have the money to book a hotel room. You can like and care about someone wholeheartedly, but if they come around or show interest in you only when it is convenient to them, they are not worth your time.

Weeks later, I again saw Mark waiting across from Abbie's school. I came out of the bus and again hid myself. This time, anticipating the direction he would take, I made my way into the town where I concealed myself at a storefront. I do not know why I even cared, but I waited to see if he would walk down the street with Abbie like he had previously done. In the distance, I could see them coming. Mark had his hands around her shoulders. My heart melted. The tears dripped. I placed myself behind a parked car in front of the store, and as they passed, I sneaked out and sank my fist into Abbie's back. She spun around, and we approached each other ready to engage in combat. The crowd gathered, eager to witness the family feud unfolding before them. Some started cheering us on to fight. She did not return the blow, but instead a word battle ensued.

"You're such a fool," she shouted, as she made her way towards me.

"Stop running after other people's husbands," I yelled back. "Get your own."

"Look at me, and look at you!" she said as her hands caressed the frame of her body. "All the men want me! Even your husband wants me— you skinny whip!"

Hoping to validate my actions before the crowd and let them understand that I had full rights to the scuffle, I shamelessly yelled back, "Stop messing with my husband! You are messing with a married man!"

With the word battle in full swing, Mark stood and looked on. He must have felt like a king. After a while he walked up to me and shouted, "You put me out! Why do you even care what I'm doing? Go home and stop embarrassing yourself and embarrassing me." With those words he walked back to Abbie, and together they walked away. I walked up the street sobbing uncontrollably and feeling sorry for myself. This was not the man I married. Something had gone terribly wrong. I felt alone and rejected. The hurt was too much to bear.

I had hoped that by now I would have gotten over Mark, but each time I saw him, especially with Abbie, I was hurt all over again. I began to feel extreme anger and hatred towards him. I saw him as the root of all my pain and suffering, and at times, I wished he were dead. I should have sought help, but I didn't, and as a result, I made some very poor choices that I gravely regret to this day. I never believed in repaying evil with evil or holding grudges in my heart for those who had done me wrong, but I threw these convictions out the door because I was overwhelmed by the hurt I was experiencing. I made the choice not to forgive Mark, and the more I harbored hatred towards him, the longer the pain lingered. By harboring hatred in my heart, I was doing myself no good, for I became extremely anxious and extremely depressed. I should have focused more on the positive aspects of my life, but instead, I chose to focus on the negative because of my dwindling faith in God. I had fallen in a pit of despair, and He seemed to leave me there.

As time went on, I continued to glimpse Mark in the town, and I felt sure he had come to visit Abbie. I forced myself to accept that our relationship was over, but this was very difficult because apart from having a son together, I carried a part of him inside of me. He showed no interest in the baby. In fact, he averted all talk about the pregnancy. He occasionally showed up at my door and asked to see his son or at times to speak to me, but he would never mention the pregnancy. I suspected that Abbie, too, was carrying Mark's baby. This was excruciatingly painful. Some nights I lay under the covers and cried myself to sleep. It seemed impossible to surmount the hurt I was feeling. Each time I saw Mark or glimpsed Abbie in the town, the hurt resurfaced, causing me to relive the experience mentally and emotionally.

Day after day, I developed an uncontrollable urge to hurt Abbie. I hated that this marauder stole Mark's love away from me and my unborn baby. One day, I glimpsed her going into a bus, and I again ran toward her and punched her in her back. She looked around debating whether to come after me but continued into the bus. In my immaturity and insecurity, I directed my rage toward her because I unjustly deemed her the perpetrator in the affair. This was a bad idea because by constantly attacking her, I was revealing my weakness and giving her power over me.

From courtship to very early in our marriage, Mark had been my happiness, my everything. He was constantly on my mind. Sometimes I would sit silently and allow my mind to wander about our happy moments. More than anything else in the world, I wanted to make him happy. Early in our courtship, I came to the realization that Mark was deficient in his ability to read and write effectively. He was a little less schooled than I was. I found this out when Mark first wrote me a letter. In the letter, he wrote a story about a woman who had found a pig wallowing in the mud, taken it home, cleaned it up, and allowed it to be a part of her home. After a while, the pig became tired of trying to be who it was not and ran away. It returned to wallowing in the mud. Even though most of the words were misspelled in the letter, I chose to help Mark rather than shun him. I always believed that true love was all about helping your partner grow, so I was happy to help, and because he wanted to learn, we spent numerous hours of our courtship reading to enhance his literacy skills. With all this history between us, I thought that our love was unbreakable.

The truth of the matter is that the pure love I thought I had for Mark was really infatuation. I had allowed myself to become entwined in an emotional love affair which resulted in a toxic, codependent relationship in which Mark sat on the throne of my heart even amid the hurt he was dishing out. Each time I saw him with Abbie, I felt wounded and crushed but still had difficulty letting go and moving on with my life. I had become so enmeshed in the relationship that I lost my sense of self, my own distinctiveness. I did not know how to live my life without him. I did not know how to continue my life along a happy and healthy path. I felt worthless. I had spent my married life helping Mark to create his own value, yet I did not even know how to appreciate and see value in myself. I began to hate myself for what had been done to me. I want you to know that when you lose your sense of self, and you no longer see your worth, you are more inclined to accept mistreatment and abuse from your spouse. You are more inclined to blame yourself for all that's going wrong in the relationship. I had placed Mark on the throne of my heart, and when he failed, I saw myself as a failure. I had idolized my marriage, and when it crumbled, I too crumbled. Remember, we can turn the beautiful gift of marriage into something bad if we take God off His throne and place someone or something else upon it. Only God deserves to be on the throne of our hearts and our lives. Idolizing my spouse and my marriage came with a cost, and to pay, I sacrificed my relationship with God.

Twelve

HIS MIGHTY HANDS

WHEN I THINK ABOUT the depth to which I had fallen, I feel very ashamed. I had never been the type that would plot to hurt someone, and I had never been the type to be physically violent towards another, but I had allowed myself to become so consumed by my own emotions and the stresses of life that I became emotionally and spiritually dry. I was numb! Each day I experienced chronic feelings of emptiness and feelings of emotional numbness and despair. Love, peace, and self-control used to be the embodiment of my life, but now hatred, anger, and instability took over. Deep inside, I knew that that was not the true me. I was changing. I was moving away from God. Unfortunately, I had sought fulfillment in marriage, and when that did not work out, I became angry, very angry. Had I known then that true fulfillment does not come from marriage or any earthly entity, my circumstances would have been different. True fulfillment can only come from God, for He alone can fill the void in our lives. If only I had allowed Him in, instead of shutting Him out, my life would have taken on new meaning.

Months passed, and I felt sure that by now I would have gotten over Mark. I wanted him to be history, completely out of my life, but each time I spotted him in the town, the hurt resurfaced, and I had no doubt he was still seeing Abbie. I spent countless hours during the night flipping through the wedding album in tears. I used to think that we were a match made in heaven, and each time I flipped through the album, I became angry thinking about how Mark had ruined it all. He turned my dream into a nightmare. Why couldn't Mark keep a simple promise to be faithful? Each time I beheld my swollen face and reddened eyes in the wedding pictures, I could not help but see it as a clear sign of warning. As I walked down the aisle that day, I had no clue that I would spend a major part of my marriage with a swollen face and reddened eyes from constant crying. My heart was permanently aching. I was filled with grief and pain.

Falling victim to infidelity can be a very degrading and defeating experience that leaves you feeling inadequate and unworthy. Your feelings of inadequacy and unworthiness can then incite self-defeating thoughts. You might think that your spouse went on the outside because the other person was either more attractive or more sexually appealing than you. You might think that your chance of being happy or fulfilled has been obliterated because your spouse cheated on you. You might view yourself as the loser in the struggle that existed within the relationship, and this prolongs feelings of defeat. These self-defeating thoughts can then lead to self-destructive behaviors. Picture yourself driving a car, and suddenly it begins to spin out of control. You can try to control it, or you can decide the struggle is not worth it, take your hands off the steering wheel, and let it crash. When life begins to spin out of control, there are some who give up thinking that their life is not worth fighting for. This can be a very dangerous situation with dangerous consequences if no help is sought.

One night, I lay in bed crying. My mind was overrun with self-defeating thoughts. Scenes of the past involuntarily raced through my mind. I recalled the day I confronted Abbie and Mark in the town. All efforts to dismiss those thoughts failed. In my mind, I could see her hands caress the frame of her body as she said, "Look at me and look at you! All the men want me! Even your husband wants me— you skinny whip!" Her words indicated that I was less shapely than she was, and she was just the right size for Mark. The scene was being replayed over and over in my mind making it impossible for me to fall asleep.

As other past events flashed through my mind, I began to feel more and more worthless, and I began to verbalize even more self-defeating thoughts such as: "I hate myself," "I am ugly," "I'm a failure." Involuntary thoughts kept flashing through my mind, and I fought desperately to drive them out, but they lingered. I felt hopeless. I was that car spinning out of control. I was the one fighting desperately to control it and realizing it was a losing battle. I was about to take my hands off the steering and let it crash. Life was not worth this struggle! Life was not worth fighting for. I wished to escape my inward turmoil. I did not want to live anymore. I looked up from under the covers at the clock in front of me, my eyes blurry with tears. It was about 9:00 PM. I got out the bed and made a few steps toward the kitchen.

Right then, I heard someone knocking on my door. Standing outside was my sister-in-law, my mom, and my son. I quickly wiped away the tears, opened the door, and let them in. My sister-in-law ran and hugged me. She was married to Mark's brother. She was near to tears as she said, "Karen, I had to come and look for you." I tried desperately to fall asleep but could not fall asleep. You were on my mind. Something was pressing me to come and check on you." She lived on the same street with my mom, so she woke my mom up to accompany her to my home. My mom woke up my son and brought him along, thinking it would be nice for me to see him. My sister-in-law looked at me and said, "You're not staying here by yourself. Pack your clothes. You're leaving with us!"

I complied, knowing that the scene that just played out before me was a definite act of God. I packed my things, and I left to spend some time with my son and my mom.

From time to time, we go through rough patches in our lives, and because the load seems too heavy to bear, we feel inclined to give up. Are you going through a difficult situation? Do you feel like giving up? Wait! Hear me out. Think about the story of the Children of Israel for a second. They endured years of bondage and oppression at the hands of the Egyptians. They sought God's help, and in His own time He delivered them. Oh, how they longed for that day when they would be free from captivity and free from oppression. They must have looked forward to a life of bliss in the Promised Land. Unbeknown to them, they were to spend 40 years wandering through the wilderness. It was a difficult 40 years, but God brought them through. It was in those years they learned resilience, reliance, and providence. In the wilderness, they developed spiritual fortification, learned to depend on God every step of the way, and experienced the divine interventions of God. God can use our rough patches to teach us resilience, reliance, and providence also.

The rough patches in your life might just be your wilderness experience. I want you to know that you are not alone. God is right there in the wilderness with you. He is touched by your aching heart. He is touched by your sleepless nights of crying. There is no sorrow, no heartache, no anguish to which He turns a blind eye. Whatever the difficulty, He feels what you feel. Hang in there! I want you to know that weeping may endure for a night, but joy comes in the morning. Don't lose hope. There is a better day coming. Yes, you will have difficult moments and experiences. Yes, you will have weeping, but take comfort in knowing that your weeping will one day go away. Joy will come in the morning. No one knows when your morning will come, but God knows! Trust Him to work things out for you in His time. I couldn't see it then, and perhaps you're having a hard time seeing it now, but take it from me: It may seem as though He has abandoned you, but be patient because He hasn't! He never does! He may not show up when you want Him to, but I can assure you, He always shows up just in time. Ask Him for the strength to make it through. In our strength we fail, but in His strength, we prevail. Put your hands in His, and He will walk with you each step of the way.

Your wilderness experience can be a learning experience. Seek to learn from it and grow through it. It will help you develop a stronger character and lead you toward spiritual maturity. Remember, the testing of your faith produces steadfastness.

> A gem cannot be polished without friction nor man without trials. —Chinese Proverb.

Give yourself a chance, and you will survive your experience. You will walk out of your wilderness as a man or a woman of substance, and you will be better equipped to enter the Promised Land. In your possession will be an even greater testimony designed to help others escape their darkness and step boldly into the light. I urge you, do not give up. In my wilderness experience, I almost gave up, but thank God, He placed His hands on my hands and kept them on the steering wheel. Thank God I am here today to share my testimony with you.

Footprints in the Sand

One night I dreamed a dream.
As I was walking along the beach with my Lord.
Across the dark sky flashed scenes from my life.
For each scene, I noticed two sets of footprints in the sand,
One belonging to me and one to my Lord.

After the last scene of my life flashed before me,
I looked back at the footprints in the sand.
I noticed that at many times along the path of my life,
especially at the very lowest and saddest times,
there was only one set of footprints.

This really troubled me, so I asked the Lord about it.
"Lord, you said once I decided to follow you,
You'd walk with me all the way.
But I noticed that during the saddest and most troublesome times of my life,
there was only one set of footprints.
I don't understand why, when I needed You the most, You would leave me."

He whispered, "My precious child, I love you and will never leave you
Never, ever, during your trials and testings.
When you saw only one set of footprints,
It was then that I carried you."

—Unknown

Thirteen

AUTHENTIC VS INAUTHENTIC REPENTANCE

THE BEST THING ABOUT repentance is the change that results from a broken spirit and a broken and contrite heart. If your contrition does not elicit a change in behavior, your repentance is of non-effect. As you allow God to take you off the old path and place you on a new path, you will willingly admit and take responsibility for your wrongdoings instead of making excuses for them; you will confess your wrongdoings despite the consequences you may face; you will do all that lie in your power to make amends and demonstrate your change; and you will seek professional help, if necessary, to help you stay on the right path. You see, true repentance is not merely ceasing our walk down the old beaten path of sin. It is making a 180 degree turn back into the arms of God after we have strayed away from Him. It is placing ourselves at His feet, humbling ourselves before Him, admitting our guilt and wrongdoing, and allowing Him to lead us every step of the way on our new journey. It is asking Him for strength to remain on the right path and believing that He will be with us, every step of the way.

The few times I spoke to Mark during our separation, he never demonstrated a spirit of repentance. He never admitted to doing wrong. Much of what took place on that fateful day was my fault. In fear of how I would react, he dragged Abbie into the bedroom that day. Because of my dramatic reaction, Abbie was forced to escape through the bedroom window. I ask too many questions, and this causes him to tell lies. Knowing that Mark was not repentant, when I received a call from the pastor a few months into our separation, I should have disregarded his attempts to speak with Mark and me. He was the minister who facilitated our marriage vows, and when he heard about our separation, he thought he could do something to help. In his call, he asked me to meet him at Mark's parents' home. Having such respect for him made it difficult for me to deny his request, so I promised him I would be there. I immediately made my way there. As the minister spoke to us, Mark continued to deny most of the allegations I made against him. We went through several hours of counseling. The minister brought a young man with him who confessed to me that he, too, had cheated on his wife, but God had helped him to change. He was very passionate about the subject of forgiveness because of the life he had lived and the deliverance he was able to achieve.

"You should give him another chance," the young man said. "If I can change, anyone can."

I smiled, but I knew within my heart that the two situations were different. Maybe the young man was truly repentant, but Mark was not. I didn't even get the sense that he was being truthful to the minister when he said that he was willing to give our marriage a second shot. Mark was still denying his infidelity, and this to me was mind-boggling. I really wanted to walk out of the house and let them all know that it was over between Mark and me, but I did not know how to do it. I looked at Mark's mother's face, and my heart melted. Since Mark and I separated, she would frequently come to my home and cry because of what had happened to Mark and me. His sister, too, was standing a little way off. I thought about how she and Mark's mom had visited me and asked me to take them to Abbie's parent's home. They had gone there to beg Abbie to stop destroying Mark's family, and in my mind, I could still see the hurt and disappointment on their faces as they returned from their discourse that no doubt was fruitless. Now their faces beamed with hope, hope of a reconciliation. Hope that everything would return to normal for Mark and me. I felt very unsettled. There I was, sitting with the minister and Mark, unsure of what to do. I remembered the many sermons I heard in church about how God hates divorce. I felt that my hesitancy was making God sad. With so many emotions running high, even though I was not fully convinced that Mark was repentant, I agreed to renew my vows with him.

I was already in the process of selling my house, and I let Mark know that. I had plans to move closer to my mom. A man I knew was selling a plot of land not too far from my mom, so I decided to purchase it from him to rebuild a home. At first, I did not let Mark know that I had plans to rebuild a home because I wasn't sure if things would work out between us. I was moving closer to my mom because she had promised to help with the kids until things stabilized with me. My mom was my help and confidant who knew what I was going through and was always there to help. She never meddled or said anything to Mark about how he was treating me, but she constantly reminded me to pray. She truly believed that if I earnestly petitioned God, He could turn Mark around and bring him to his knees in repentance. This I did; however, while praying for Mark to change, I neglected to pray for myself. It wasn't only Mark who needed to change; I needed to change also. I needed to restore my relationship with God and resolve the anger I felt toward Him for not protecting me from the hurt I was going through. I needed to open my heart to Him, invite Him in, and return to loving and serving Him the way I previously did, but no, I was so focused on Mark and the hurt I was experiencing that I failed to see what I needed. I needed God! Only He could provide me with the wisdom, courage, strength, and faith that I needed to survive the long and difficult journey I was about to embark upon.

    Mark moved back into the home. Everything went okay for a while, and Mark and I tried to make our marriage work. He tried to convince me that he no longer spoke to Abbie, but it was difficult for me to trust him knowing I had been lied to so many times before. After all that Mark had done to me, I knew it would take a lot of work to bring things back the way it used to be. All the things Mark had put me through had affected me in more ways than anyone can imagine. I was always on edge; my mind was always racing; and I was always wondering where he was and what he was doing. If Mark was not at home when I returned from work, I became very uneasy and sometimes went back into the town to see if I saw him with Abbie. I would walk through the mall, look in restaurants, and conceal myself in storefronts, all in an effort to determine if he was still cheating.

It was a miserable life to live. There were times when I was almost certain that I saw them sitting together, and as I approached, it was a different couple. There were times I entered a bus and felt sure I had seen them, and as I looked closer it was not them. From a distance, every couple looked like Mark and Abbie. My mind began to play tricks on me, and I became very depressed and unhappy. Mark's affair was driving me crazy. I was not sleeping properly, and I was not eating well. I thought I would have been able to forgive him, but it now seemed impossible.

Mark was not attending church anymore. He blamed me for his refusal, claiming that had I not told everyone about his actions, it would have been easier for him to continue going. I was to blame for everything in Mark's life. Mark knew full well that he could not face the congregation after what he had done. He was well respected by the young people in our church, and his behavior shocked most of them. They admired how well he could expound upon the Bible, and how well he could defend his belief, and none of them thought him capable of what I had said he had done. A few of the adults suspected that Mark was living a double life but did not stop him from conducting the Bible class because they did not have the proof. Now that the evidence surfaced, he was ashamed to show his face. Sometimes my son and I attended by ourselves, and sometimes we stayed at home. I started to avoid church members because in their presence I was overwhelmed with self-defeating thoughts. Though I did nothing wrong, I felt unworthy and ashamed because of what Mark had done to me. Though I sat in church, my mind was not in it. I was forever thinking about Mark and wondering whether he had sneaked out to go and see Abbie. My mind was always racing, making it quite difficult to concentrate on the service, so rather than battle with these thoughts and feelings, I sometimes stayed away.

I finally found a buyer for the house, and we moved into an apartment close to my mom's house. Things began to improve after we moved. Mark and I started attending a different church, and he returned to doing electrical work. I was happy for this oasis in my life. I could not stop thanking God for what He had done for Mark and me. Soon the baby arrived, and we were happy. The nursery was fully decorated with a crib and matching chest of drawers. A beautiful pink sheet-set and matching pillows accentuated the space. Pink balloons, a "Welcome Home" sign, and an "It's a Girl" poster welcomed her arrival. She was a welcomed addition to the home. We all loved her. Mark would sing to her and spin her around just like he did our son. I was so happy that things were finally getting back to normal. He was doing so well finding work that I began to trust him once again.

He continued to attend church, and once again, he became actively involved in the Bible class. I found a builder to build the house, and soon it was finished. Ten months later, I was pregnant with my third child.

Mark returned to taxi driving, promising that things would be different. I trusted him to do right this time like he had promised. For a while, everything seemed to be working out as planned. He was helping with the bills, spending more time with the kids, and trying his best to help me renew my trust in him. Within a matter of months, things took a downward turn. The same thing started happening all over again. Mark started coming home later and later with little money to show for his late work. He was mainly hanging out and enjoying his life, and the responsibility of paying the bills and buying all the groceries once again rested upon me. Once again, he became full of excuses and full of lies.

How could I fall prey to this a second time? How could I be such a fool once more? Trouble had struck its ugly head again, and the news of Mark's infidelity started pouring in once more. One day a letter appeared in my mom's mailbox telling of Mark's affairs. In fact, according to the claim, his affairs had never stopped. The letter revealed that he had two additional babies with two different women, and now he was seeing someone else. I knew that Mark had gone off the deep end, but I did not fathom that he had fallen so deep. Once again, my heart was writhing in pain. The letter revealed that he had had one baby with Abbie and the other with GeGe, a lady I met a few times in his taxi and who had previously come to our gate to show Mark her baby.

She had placed the baby in Mark's arms, and in my mind, I did question that gesture and secretly wondered what the connection was between herself, Mark, and the baby.

When I approached Mark about the letter he said, "Whoever wrote that letter is lying. They are trying to get you to put me out again."

By now I was unequivocally able to finish Mark's thoughts. I guess whoever wrote the letter was jealous of us. They would go to every length to break up our marriage. It was all a hoax. I had heard those words too many times over the years. I knew Mark was lying. He never told the truth. Now I understood why he looked so nervous the day GeGe came to our gate. That baby was his child. He continued to deny all allegations thrown at him:

"I have no other children but these here! I have no idea what you're talking about!"

The drama Mark brought was too much to bear. I should have removed myself from the situation but felt inclined to stay and suck it up for the children's sake. I had two children, and now another one was on the way, and this made it a little more difficult to walk away. Additionally, I was embarrassed to admit to others that my marriage, the perfect marriage I had sought, had failed. I was in great emotional pain, and I had to force myself to go on, yet I stayed. Each time I built up hope, Mark tore it down. I was afraid to hope. I was afraid to trust. I was afraid to leave. Amid the pain and the turmoil, my third child arrived, and I thanked God for her. I asked God to give me the strength to take care of my children and to prevent them from becoming indirect victims of what I was going through.

Mark and I continued to attend church, but this time, I did not tell anyone at church about my plight. I sucked it up alone because I did not want to be the reason Mark stopped going to church again. I did not want anyone to ask me about our relationship, so I faked happiness in their presence.

Sadly, I was still trying to adorn a marriage that was already covertly scarred. I resented Mark for this. He had ruined my life. Just the sight of him brought so much pain. My head and my heart were constantly aching. How could one human being be so deceitful? To see him sit in church and act like a saint was beyond my comprehension. To see him stand before the congregation and conduct Bible classes was mind-boggling. To see him sit on the rostrum and take his place at the podium and pretend that everything was hunky-dory with his life was very frustrating. I regularly sat in church with a heart full of pain, yet no one noticed. No one knew that the sister who regularly walked through the doors of the church was walking around with a heart full of pain, sadness, and despair!

Fourteen

OFF THE DEEP END

IN TODAY'S SOCIETY, THERE are some who claim to be followers of God, yet they live in sin and commit sinful acts. In their quest to appear righteous in the eyes of the masses, they choose to cover up their sins instead of repenting from them. They ignore God's call to repentance. "If we confess our sins, he is faithful and just to forgive us our sins, and to cleanse us from all unrighteousness" (I John 1:9).

Rather than repent from his sins, Mark took the difficult road of covering them up. He gave little regard to the consequences of his actions and the ripples of effects that resulted from them. No one should disregard the fact that one wrongdoing can affect numerous people for a very long time. The story is told of an ant and an elephant who got into a fight one day, and the ant managed to kill the elephant. The ant grew up in a moral society, so he became fearful for the consequences of his action. That is when he decided to dig a hole around and under to bury the elephant. The ant, unfortunately, spent the rest of his life digging. The repercussions of our wrongdoing can last for months, years, and yes, even a lifetime. Additionally, innocent lives can be impacted.

Mark gave little regard to his actions and the impact it was having on his family. Not only was he hurting me, but he was hurting his children, too. They rarely saw him, for he often came home late at night when they were already asleep. They often saw me crying, and it became customary for them to ask, as they dried my tears away, "Why is daddy making you cry?" Children, regardless of how young, do not like to see a parent hurt. It makes them distrust others and can affect their future relationships. They may think that if their daddy whom they love so much can hurt their mom, and vice versa, then anyone else, including their daddy, may hurt them. For their sakes, I tried to stop myself from crying. I hated that they were privy to my suffering, but at times I could not conceal my hurt. I thought about how I was privy to my mom's suffering and how it was devastating to me. Oh, how I wished that things had been different for them.

I concluded that Mark might never change because he was contented with the way he lived. He was a thrill seeker who created a fan club of admirers, lovers, and potential lovers to harness his sexual fantasies. All the while, he hung around hoping that I would be his main source. He enjoyed the thrill and was not ready to give up the gratification his sexual conquest brought. No one would have guessed that Mark was like that. He duped everyone into believing that he was charming, upright, and moral. He undoubtedly duped me also. During courtship and the first three years of our marriage, I would have risked my life to defend

Mark's character. Back then I viewed him as a spiritually and morally minded young man who practiced what he preached. The revelation of Mark's destructive and deceptive trajectory came as a shock to me. I would have never guessed that he was like that and would have been upset with anyone who tried to convince me otherwise. Mark betrayed me! His betrayal was not an isolated event but a habitual treachery that went on for years and years— a classic betrayal! He lied his way through it all. Sometimes he got caught and sometimes he did not, and it was clear that he did not mind the drama his infidelity caused. Like a hunter in pursuit of game, he went from woman to woman. Except for my first, each time I was pregnant, another woman was pregnant with one of his babies as well. Thanks to the informants who brought his darkness into the light. Today I still do not know the identity of the bearer of the letters that were twice hand delivered into my mother's mailbox. Tidings of despair, I call them. As to why he or she chose to involve my mom, I may never know, but each time they came, my mom allowed me to read them. Those letters let me know that Mark was having affairs with multiple women throughout our marriage. Every read was a painful experience. Every read was heartbreaking.

Mark was so clever in manipulating my reality that, as time went on, I began to question the reality of everything in my life. Nothing seemed real, and nothing made sense anymore. I had been lied to so many times that I began to second-guess myself even when the truth was so glaring. Despite finding Abbie in my bedroom, despite GeGe bringing the baby to our gate, despite all the women I knew of, he was adamant that he was never unfaithful to me. He was adamant that none of the alleged babies were his. I found myself going through bouts of confusion and self-doubt. Despite what I learned from his friends and his family, I questioned myself and wondered if I was imagining it all. What a sad place to be! One by one, these women entered my life as boastful and daring contenders. I came home one day to find GeGe and her daughter hanging out with Mark and my children in my driveway while he washed the taxi. I appeared unexpectedly on the taxi stand one day and little did I know that the woman standing next to me was the new perpetrator, Val, whom one of the letters mentioned. When he drove up, his taxi was empty, and both of us entered. He was nervous and introduced Val as a friend. He claimed that he was on his way to the mechanic. She deceitfully rode along with Mark and me to the mechanic, claiming to be just a friend.

The hurt kept on coming. Day after day they came and would not let up. I started experiencing chest pains and palpitations, but for the children's sake and to save the face of my marriage, I stayed. Though I was losing my mind, I stayed. My diminishing self-confidence, my increasing self-doubt, and Mark's manipulation tactics made it quite easy for me to remain in this emotionally and psychologically abusive relationship. Believe it or not, there were days when I still saw Mark as gentle, charming, caring, understanding, and affectionate. I was becoming so used to his abuse that his behaviors seemed normal. Mark's favorite accusation against me was that I wanted to keep him in a cage, but no, I was the one in the cage. I was an emotional hostage in our relationship. I was the one held captive for years. I should have walked away many years ago, but I did not. Why? Because I was afraid. I had become so emotionally dependent upon Mark that I was not sure how to live my life without him. I needed to walk out of the relationship from a place of strength but was devoid of it, so in my weakness, I felt compelled to stay.

Mark continued to go to church and pretend that everything was okay even though he was living a reckless life for someone who had made a marital commitment. For some reason, he began to act as though he was still a teenager and not a grown man now in his thirties with three children, or more for that matter. He was still hanging out with friends most of the day rather than productively working, and the financial responsibility of maintaining our home still rested mainly on me. Mark did not seem to care about the stress I was enduring while trying to make ends meet and upkeep our home. He did not seem to care that I was hurting because of all that he had put me through. He refused to agree to marital counseling and remained firm that it was unnecessary because nothing was wrong with our marriage and none of the allegations against him were true. His constant denial and his manipulation contributed to me living a lonely and empty life for several years.

I was about 30 when my health began to deteriorate. Thank God I was offered an opportunity to take voluntary separation from my job. I began to experience severe headaches, palpitations, and chest pains. Day after day, I would stand before my open window, peer into the sky, and ask God, *Why? Why did my life turn out like this? Why couldn't Mark just change his way of life? If not for me, why couldn't he change for Him and for the children?* I pleaded with Mark to change his way of life, but he was content to live according to the flesh. Mark knew that God could help him live above sin, but he liked what he was doing and was not ready to put his sin to death. I came to understand the meaning of the story that he wrote to me at the onset of our relationship. The pig was taken out of the mud, cleaned up, and allowed to be a part of the woman's home. After a while, the pig got fed up with being who it was not. It ran away and returned to wallowing in the mud. Maybe Mark was sending a message. Maybe he thought he was doomed to a life in the mud—a life controlled by sinful passions. The truth of the matter is: No one is doomed to a life of sin and passion. There is hope in God. "Therefore if any man be in Christ, he is a new creature: old things are passed away; behold, all things are become new" (2 Cor 5: 17). I pleaded to God to change Mark, but my prayers went unanswered.

Fifteen

FIGHT OR FLIGHT

MONTHS WENT BY, AND I found myself remaining more and more in the bed. I was in a constant state of worry, fear, and dread that left me tired all the time. I was constantly nervous. I had a prolonged tingling in my arms and legs and sometimes felt a sudden tightness in my neck, shoulder, and my lower back, a tightness that made it difficult for me to turn from side to side. I could sense that something was not normal with my body. One day I was on a bus taking my son to the doctor for a preoperative visit when suddenly my body began to shake, a sensation of tightness arose in my shoulders and in my back, and my heart began to race. It happened suddenly. I became very fearful. I felt like I was dying. I rang the bell to alert the driver that I was having an emergency. The driver pulled aside on the busy highway and came to see what was wrong. I was shaking incessantly. Everyone in the bus looked on, terrified.

"What's wrong?" asked the driver.

I could hardly respond because I could barely breathe. Still shaking, I responded, "I need some water."

Someone in the bus offered me a bottle of water. I gobbled it down, and after a few minutes, the feeling subsided. I was very fearful and afraid that it would happen again, but I made it to the doctor's office. I could not figure out what had just happened. I was afraid to ride the bus back home, for fear it would happen again. Thank God my son and I made it home safely. This was the beginning of another trouble that would linger with me for years. I went from doctor to doctor to try to determine what was wrong, but no doctor could tell me what was happening to my body. It reached the point where I barely left the house, for every time I attempted, I could only make a few steps before my heart began to race and my chest tightened up. I became like a prisoner trapped in my own body and trapped in my home. I would get up in the morning feeling nauseous and awake during the night feeling dizzy. I was always feeling anxious, and my mind was always racing.

As time went on, I had severe difficulty falling asleep. Thinking about Mark's behavior did not help, for whenever I thought about it, my body went into a state of panic that happens like this: For no apparent reason, I begin to feel fearful. A tight sensation arises in my shoulders and in my back, and my heart begins to race. I begin to feel lightheaded and nauseous, and I feel as if I am being smothered. My chest begins to squeeze together, I begin to cold sweat, and my muscles begin to twitch. I feel like I am losing control, and it becomes difficult to walk because I can barely breathe. All this takes place in a matter of five to fifteen minutes. It then subsides, and with every passing minute, I become more and more fearful, because I am afraid that it will happen again. That became the story of my life. These attacks would come on suddenly, and after a while, they began to come on regularly. It was like a fight or flight response repeatedly triggered for no apparent reason. This became my new normal. Not only was I losing control of my mind, now I was losing control of my body!

I spent most of my waking hours in the bed. This was very sad because I had previously left my job to take care of my kids, and now I could barely take care of them. I felt drained. I was caught in a vicious cycle of infidelity, constantly being hurt, and the burden became too heavy to bear. I needed help! I went from doctor to doctor, trying to find out what was wrong with me, and no one seemed to be able to help. Test after test was done and all came back negative. I felt helpless. I felt hopeless. My illness did not seem to bother Mark, who claimed I was making myself sick. The loving caring Mark I once knew in courtship and early marriage had totally disappeared. I fought to keep myself together, and I tried not to regress into being angry with God. I had a few good days in between, but the majority were quite difficult. I tried to dismiss Mark and his lifestyle out of my thoughts, but they coerced themselves in, and each time they came in, the symptoms lingered.

The more the news kept coming about Mark's infidelity, the more the symptoms came on. I became almost bedridden. I was afraid to get out of bed for fear of getting an attack.

Since the doctors could not detect any physical ailment, they passed it off as stress. I tried desperately to focus on the positive aspects of my life, but each time the negatives drowned them out. Mark continued to come home in the wee hours of the morning; news was still pouring in about his infidelity; he was still denying all the allegations; and he continued to conduct the Bible class as though he was doing nothing wrong. It was now years, and nothing changed with Mark.

The more I worried about my situation, the more I became ill. My body was constantly shaking, and my brain felt congested. On some days, my speech became slurred, and my heart would suddenly skip beats. The only place I found relief was in the bed and sometimes at church. If my good days fell on the weekend, I would go to church, hoping that the fellowship, the singing, and the praying would bring me some relief. These helped to some extent. It was a joy just to know that I made it out of the house. I did not feel comfortable being in crowded places, so I usually sat all the way to the back. Whenever people came around to greet me, I felt very shaky, my head felt full, and my eyes went dim. I could not understand why these feelings suddenly appeared. I became quite uncomfortable when others looked directly at me because I was almost certain that they were seeing what I felt. This made me more anxious, brought on self-pity, and intensified the attacks. Sometimes when I tried to sing, I would experience shortness of breath, and if the service was loud, I had no choice but to leave. Loud noises sometimes triggered the attack. This situation left me feeling very miserable and sorry for myself.

There were days when my worries did not consume me, and I appeared to get some relief, but as soon as thoughts of Mark's infidelity crossed my mind, the symptoms reappeared. I had no energy to even complete my usual chores. I would do light things inside the house, but frequently I would experience palpitations and extreme shortness of breath that would force me right back to the bed. I had no appetite and sometimes had to struggle to swallow my food. As a result, I was losing weight. These symptoms made me very fearful and left me feeling despondent. I had difficulty sleeping, and many nights, I did not blink an eye. Luckily, my mom moved in to assist me. On the nights I could not sleep, she stayed awake with me and tried to comfort me. At times I saw her crying. I am sure she wanted to be strong for me, but to witness what I was going through must have been heartbreaking.

There were times I tried to leave home, but after walking a few blocks the symptoms would intensify, causing me to return to the house; however, I never gave up on trying. On one of my good days, I made it to the town. My mom and my children accompanied me. Everything was going well when amid my shopping, my heart began to race, my body began to shake, and I began gasping for breath. This was difficult for my children to experience. I found somewhere to sit and then after several minutes, the symptoms subsided. I had to cut my shopping and hurry back to the house because I was always afraid that the attack would happen again.

This went on for about two years. I went to various doctors trying to find out what was wrong with me, and none could tell me what was happening to my body. A close friend referred me to a doctor that she said would probably be able to help. I made an appointment to see him. As I was getting dressed that morning, I could feel the symptoms intensifying, but I continued to get dressed. The radio was on, and someone was talking. His words suddenly caught my attention: "No one is worth dying for." I sat down and the words resounded in my ears. "No one is worth dying for." I thought about my condition and developed an even greater determination to do something about it.

As I developed the will power, I could feel the symptoms subsiding. I made it to the doctor alone. This was the first doctor to address the root of the problem. He wanted to know everything, and I felt safe to speak freely. I told him everything. He helped me to see that what I was going through was psychological. He asked me a pertinent question.

"Do you love yourself?"

I cried because deep down inside I knew that my actions were saying no. He advised me to go back to loving myself and taking care of myself. He gave me strategies to identify and re-channel the negative thoughts that were plaguing my mind and triggering the attacks. He also gave me a list of physical and breathing exercises to enhance relaxation. At the end of the visit, he asked me if I had any family in the United States of America. I told him I had two sisters who lived there. He advised me to take a vacation and spend some "me" time.

"You have to start back living," he said. "Find things you enjoy, and do them."

The words of the radio host kept resounding in my ears. "No one is worth dying for!" That was motivating. Prior to visiting the doctor, my sister had invited me to her wedding in the U.S., and thinking it impossible to travel to the United States of America with everything I was going through, I told her I could not attend. The doctor's plea along with the radio host's words pushed me to go straight to a travel agency and book a flight to the United States of America.

Sixteen

OUT OF THE MIRY CLAY

I CAME TO THE REALIZATION that I had to do something about my situation. I was on the edge of a precipice, about to fall off. Something had to be done. I had stopped living. I was just existing. I had allowed my fears, pain, and hurt to consume me and deplete my mental well-being, leaving me in a state of helplessness and hopelessness. I died emotionally and spiritually, and now I was dying psychologically. The words of the radio host lingered in my mind: "No one is worth dying for!" I should have known all along that no one was worth dying for— except the one true God. I cried out to God for help.

"Don't 'let me die," I begged. "My children need me. I need me."

Not only did I need me, but I also needed God! I had betrayed God by allowing Him to play second fiddle to Mark. I needed to get rid of my earthly god and recommit my life to the One True God. That earthly god had failed me repeatedly, but my Eternal God, He never fails. I asked God for forgiveness. I needed forgiveness for making Mark the center of my life and allowing him to consume my existence. I had filled my heart with so much affection for Mark that there was little room in my heart for God. When Mark failed me, I filled my heart with the hurt that so relentlessly engulfed me, and my spiritual life became stagnant. I went to church, I prayed, I studied, but my heart was not in it. I betrayed God. I should have known better because I was raised to know better. This was a classic betrayal. While Mark was betraying me, I was betraying God!

For years, I held on to the thought that if my marriage failed, I was a failure. I had allowed this thought to lock me in a constant state of sadness and despair which consequently crippled my existence. I was never one to accept defeat, so I struggled along in the marriage even though it was killing me. I wanted to win, and I fought to win despite the detrimental cost to my health and my dignity. What I wanted was not what I needed, but I was too blind to see, and too unwilling to accept. I wanted a perfect marriage, and I set out to attain it regardless of the cost, even if it meant sacrificing my deeply rooted principles to achieve it. I wanted something beautiful to measure myself by, and I sought for that beauty in marriage. I wanted the marriage to be so perfect, a monument so beautiful, that it would accentuate my life and make me feel better about myself.

I made a terrible mistake. I was too focused on what I wanted, and in my self-absorption, I paid little attention to what God wanted for me. I had spent all these years pursuing Mark when I should have been pursuing God. The Bible teaches us to "seek [pursue] first the kingdom of God, and his righteousness, and all these things [a happy and fulfilling relationship or marriage] shall be added unto you" (Matt 6: 33). I needed to empty myself and make room for God to fill me up with His goodness, mercy, and grace, for only then would I be able to let go of the things that were holding me back—inability to forgive, hatred, and self-pity. I should have laid my shortcomings and my sufferings at the feet of the Master instead of turning Him away and shutting Him out in anger. All along, He must have been sad for me, sad that I was too focused on me as a victim to behold His loving hands stretched down toward me. I was not looking up, so I could not see, and as a result, I wasted years of precious and happy moments with Him.

That night I sat on my bed and looked at the Bible on my nightstand. I opened it, and my fingers fell straight on the twentieth chapter of Psalms. I read the first few verses:

> [1] I waited patiently for the Lord; and he inclined unto me, and heard my cry.
>
> [2] He brought me up also out of an horrible pit, out of the miry clay, and set my feet upon a rock, and established my goings.
>
> [3] And he hath put a new song in my mouth, even praise unto our God: many shall see it, and fear, and shall trust in the Lord. (Ps 20: 1- 3)

I leaned back on my bed and held the Bible to my heart. I saw this as a stark reminder that I could be delivered from the pit of despair that I was so ruthlessly thrown into. It was no accident that I had encountered these words. God was speaking to me through His word. He was assuring me that He could deliver me from my illness and restore strength and vitality to my life, but I needed to let go and let Him take over. Through His word, He was inviting me into a deeper relationship with Him, a relationship that would allow me to love and serve Him honestly and wholeheartedly regardless of what I was going through. For years I had believed in a God who could take me out of any horrible situation I had found myself in, but I had allowed the agony and the degradation of my current situation to cause me to lose sight of His goodness. I was glad for the reminder that my God could restore peace and happiness to my life. I must begin by allowing Him into my life and submitting to His will and His process. His presence in my life would help me to break free from the "woe is me" mentality and restore within me a natural exuberance for life. It would put "a new song" in my mouth, a song filled with thanksgiving and praise. It would also allow me to forgive Mark even without his repentance. Mark never did his part in the forgiveness process, but I did mine to rid myself of bitterness, hate, and grudge. I knew within my heart that I had to forgive him if I wanted God to forgive me. I reached out my hands to God and as I did, I could feel His loving hands grasp mine. That day I truly felt His forgiveness, and I knew within my heart He had forgiven me for all the wrongs I had done. Is there any iniquity too big for God to forgive? No, there is none!

"If we confess our sins, he is faithful and just to forgive us our sins, and to cleanse us from all unrighteousness" (1 John 1: 9). If we come to Him with a broken and a contrite heart, He will forgive us. We do not just claim His forgiveness and continue doing the same thing. We must allow Him to change our hearts, our minds, and our actions. I claimed His forgiveness, made a commitment to live for Him, and trusted Him to do what was right for me. I knew it was not going to be an easy road, but I was determined to try.

In the morning, the symptoms were still there, but I forced myself outside and began to exercise. I walked up and down the hill to the side of my house. I was doing this for me. No longer was I going to allow myself to be held captive by Mark. No longer would I allow myself to be bombarded by fear, for fear was ruining my life—fear of failure, fear of hurt, fear of the unknown. In the evening, my children came home from school and there was an unusual smile on their faces when they saw me looking spritely and happy. I was getting ready to exercise again. They were so used to seeing me in bed that they must have been confused. I let them know that I was going to exercise. The symptoms periodically appeared, but I was not going to give up. I walked up and down the hill chanting, "I must, I must, I must improve my health!"

In the distance, I heard voices. I looked back, and it was my children walking in a straight line behind me, repeating my chant— "I must, I must, I must improve my health!"

Tears came in my eyes and there and then I knew I had to persevere. I had to do this for me, for them, for God.

Seventeen

PRESSING TOWARD THE MARK

THE TIME HAD COME for me to leave for the United States of America. I was happy and excited. I was happy because I was having better days. I was walking around, exercising, and doing my chores. Though not completely better, I knew I was making progress. I tried to dismiss fearful thoughts from infiltrating my mind by focusing more on positive thoughts, thoughts about full recovery, thoughts about the possibility of building a life for my children and me in the US, thoughts about enjoying myself at my sister's wedding. However, deep within my subconscious, I was afraid. I tried to decipher the reason for the underlying fear that hovered over me. Then it dawned upon me that I was afraid of flying by myself. I also had an underlying fear of the unknown, for I was about to take a giant step into the unknown. I wanted to leave for the U.S., not just for a vacation but for good. I did not know how that would be possible, but I knew I could not continue living the way I did. I wanted a new start in a new place. I wanted to focus on me and my recovery. I wanted to place my focus on God.

I opened my eyes to the dawn of a new day. Though still dark, little streaks of sunlight flickered through the windowpane. I lay in bed and embraced the sweet songs without. The call of frogs to their mates and the cacophony of birdsong outside the bedroom window filled the air and ignited a joy within. Their songs heralded my awakening. I sat up in bed struck by a sudden consciousness. I would soon be leaving on my journey. A sudden rush of conflicting emotions bombarded me, and as I got out of bed, I felt the symptoms coming on. I retreated to my bed. A sudden fear embraced me.

No, I am not going to let this happen, I thought to myself. I stood up, did my breathing exercises, and as light spread across the sky, I went outside to walk. I rechanneled my mind to positive things, for there was no way I was going to cancel my flight. *I will not let fear be the death of me! I will face my fears!* I remembered the words of Ralph Waldo Emerson: "Do the thing you are afraid to do and the death of fear is certain." *I will persevere, and I will be triumphant!* I told myself. After my exercise routine, I went inside, ate breakfast, spent time with my children, and then began getting ready to go to the airport. As I got dressed, I constantly reminded myself that courage was not the absence of fear, but the ability to confront it. I made a decisive effort to face my fears.

On my way to the airport, I kept telling myself that God would come through for me. "Say to them that are of a fearful heart, Be strong, fear not: behold, your God will come with vengeance, even God with a recompence; he will come and save you" (Isa 35: 4). I walked onto the tarmac and walked up the stairs getting ready to board the plane, and before reaching the top round, I looked back and gave a quick wave, a wave of goodbye. This was symbolic. I was saying goodbye to my old way of life—goodbye to broken vows and shattered dreams—goodbye to my follies, failures, frustrations, and fears. I vowed to leave them all behind. I was hopeful.

I Look Not Back

I look not back; God knows the fruitless efforts,
The wasted hours, the sinning, the regrets.
I leave them all with Him who blots the record,
And graciously forgives, and then forgets.

I look not forward; God sees all the future,
The road that, short or long, will lead me home,
And He will face with me its every trial,
And bear for me the burdens that may come.

I look not round me; then would fears assail me,
So wild the tumult of earth's restless seas,
So dark the world, so filled with woe and evil,
So vain the hope of comfort and of ease.

I look not inward; that would make me wretched;
For I have naught on which to stay my trust.
Nothing I see save failures and shortcomings,
And weak endeavors, crumbling into dust.

> But I look up--into the face of Jesus,
> For there my heart can rest, my fears are stilled;
> And there is joy, and love, and light for darkness,
> And perfect peace, and every hope fulfilled.
>
> —Annie Johnson Flint

I walked into the plane with hope, hope of a new day, hope of a new experience, hope that I would never, ever again give up on myself. I sat in my seat, and I felt the symptoms coming on. As I tried to re-channel my thoughts to things more positive, I asked God to help me not to be afraid to start all over again. There was a battle going on for my soul. Evil wanted to destroy me, but God wanted to save me. My heart began to race, and it became difficult for me to breathe. I was afraid, very afraid. My mind kept telling me that I would not be able to make the four-and-a-half-hour journey to where I was going. My mind kept telling me that I needed to get off the plane, but I prayed to God, and He strengthened my mind and gave me the confidence that I could make it. He reassured me that not only would I make it, but that He was right there holding my hands. "Be not afraid of sudden fear, neither of the desolation of the wicked, when it cometh. For the Lord shall be thy confidence..." (Prov 3: 25–26).

The plane took off into the sky, and I was gone! God held my hands through it all, and I was confident that He would give me a new life, a new experience. It may mean giving up house and vehicle, and all the material things I had accumulated for that matter. In fact, my happiness was worth much more than those. I believed that God would help me fully recover and get a job so that my children could come and be with me. I did not want to go back. I was never the one to try to escape my problems, but there comes a time when we have to say, "I have had enough!"

Being with my sisters and building a social network with newfound friends at their church helped in my recovery. Day after day, the symptoms dissipated. I was able to move around and try to find a job. This was miraculous! In less than one month, I got a job offer, which I understood to be the working hands of God. The boss offered a decent salary, so I took the job and started to save money to build a life for myself. In a few months, I bought a car and rented an apartment.

God is good. He is so compassionate, merciful, and forgiving. I ended up having to ask for God's forgiveness after allowing Mark the opportunity to come to the United States on a vacation some months later. God had delivered me from the stressful situation I was living in, yet I brought the stress to me. During his stay in the United States, Mark repeatedly used my home phone to make foreign calls to his girlfriend, Vickie, when I went to work. On one occasion, she even called the phone in my presence demanding that he send money for his baby. This was not Abbie nor GeGe nor Val. This was Vickie, someone new. Overhearing her conversation provided added evidence of his prolonged infidelity, and yet despite the conversation I overheard, he continued to lie his way out of it. I said goodbye to Mark for good. I had to leave him from a place of strength, and I thank God for finally giving me the strength.

A few months later, my children came to the United States of America. I was so happy to have them and thanked God for putting me in a position to take care of them. They mean the world to me, and I knew that I had to stay strong for them. I enrolled them in school, and they were doing great; however, I still had an issue to attend to. When you come through the immigration, you are only given permission to remain in the United States for six months. Before my first six months expired, I applied for a visa extension. Luckily enough, the immigration granted me the extension. When that six months was about to expire, in faith, I applied for another extension. I was not sure if they would grant it, but I was hopeful. Since my children were in school, I decided that it was a good time for me to go back to school; however, I had a major problem. I was still on a visitor's visa, which made me ineligible for admittance into a university. I had now been in the United States for over one year on a visitor's visa.

"How absurd," a friend said to me. "Who goes on a vacation for that long? They are not going to approve your application."

I believed in my heart that God would come through for me. I really wanted to go back to school and create a better life for myself and my children. While I waited for my second extension approval, I sought the help of a lawyer. He looked at the expiry date on my current visa and revealed that there was not enough time before the expiration to apply for a student visa. When he realized how long I had been in the

United States, he concluded that my second application for a visitor's visa extension would be denied.

"Who goes on a vacation for one and a half years?" he asked. "They are not going to approve it. You would have to return home and reapply to enter the United States." He went on to say, "If by chance your application is approved, which I don't think it will, come back to my office, and I will see what I can do for you."

His words were disappointing, but I continued to pray that God would give me an opportunity to make a life for myself and my children in the United States of America. When I arrived home, I called the phone number to check on the status of my visa extension application. The automated voice response stated that the application was still being processed. I was confused because four months had already gone by since I submitted the application. However, I still held on to the hope that the application would be approved, which would allow me time to apply for a student visa. The fact that it was still being processed was better news than to hear that my application was denied. I continued to pray to God, asking Him to come through for me. I cleared my mind and decided to stand still and see God work. This He did, for two days later when I called the number once again, the automated voice response stated that my application was approved that same day. I jumped for joy and waited patiently for the approval to come in the mail, and when it did, I hurried down to the lawyer's office to let him know that it was approved.

He looked at me in amazement and said, "You are a blessed one."

I smiled.

The lawyer advised me to go to the university that was not far from my apartment and speak to someone in the International Department.

"They will assist you in applying for a student visa," he said. I hurried on down and not only did I fill out a college application and student visa application that day, but my children were also included in the visa application process as dependents. God was miraculously working on my behalf, and I was very grateful. I continued to strengthen my relationship with Him and asked Him to show me His will for my life. Knowing the path from which I came, I knew that I had to develop the type of relationship with God, so that even if things didn't work out, I would still have faith and trust in Him. I knew I could not allow myself to fall apart when things didn't work out my way and in my time. I must believe that God knows best and has my best interest at heart. I had to remind myself of His invitation to daily bring my cares, my joys, my sorrows, and my fears to Him.

Nothing is too great for Him to bear. Nothing that concerns our peace and our well-being is too insignificant to grasp His attention. There is no fear or anxiety to which He turns a blind eye. We must exercise faith and trust in Him, for He is God, and He is good! If you are entrapped by fear and doubt, I beg you, do not lose hope. You, too, can be delivered. God is willing to help you. He will comfort, strengthen, and keep you. Yes, fears and doubts may assail you, but they do not have to be victorious over you. "For God hath not given us the spirit of fear; but of power, and of love, and of a sound mind" (2 Tim 1:7). Ask Him for strength, for in His strength, you will be victorious; you will overcome. Do not give up the fight, for there is a prize waiting for you, a prize of deliverance. Press toward the mark and claim your prize!

Eighteen

ON HIGHER GROUND

I RECEIVED THE STUDENT VISA, and I went back to school to pursue a degree in education. I have now been a teacher for over 17 years. There was a period when new stressors in my life caused the seeds of anxiety that had been planted to germinate. I sought professional help and was finally diagnosed with Generalized Anxiety Disorder, which triggered panic attacks. Unfortunately, by internalizing all my fears, hurts, and feelings of disappointments over time, I had afflicted my mind. I was placed on three different psychotropic medications. These helped for a while, but after some time the attacks intensified. After being on medication for about three years, I felt that my symptoms were worse than before I started taking them. For this reason, I decided to stop taking them. The withdrawal process was extremely difficult and lengthy during which time I developed extreme anxiety-like symptoms, but after six difficult months, I was finally set free.

Today, I am much better. I am living my life medication-free and mostly symptom-free. God has put me in a much better place and in a better frame of mind. Focusing my thoughts on things that are true, pure, and lovely help to safeguard my mind and rescue me from zones of conflict and turmoil. Over 25 years later, when Abbie's and GeGe's daughters contacted my children on social media and revealed themselves as their siblings, God kept me in perfect peace. "Thou wilt keep him in perfect peace, whose mind is stayed on thee: because he trusteth in thee" (Isa 26: 3). Instead of rubbing salt in the wound, their acknowledgement healed the wound. I am not saying that the road to recovery was easy, but I placed my focus in the right place, and God lightened the load. He was with me each step of the way. He held my hands through it all, and I am grateful!

The journey is not over. I press on each day with prayer and a determination to keep my mind fixed on God. Those who experience chronic anxiety fully understand the power that the mind has over the body and will agree with me that part of the restoration process includes restoring the mind to health. I petitioned God to be the restorer of my mind, and He took an active role in its restoration. The closer I drew to Him, the easier it became. I count on Him daily. He replaces my fears with hope, my sadness with joy, my doubts with trust, and experience has taught me to look beyond disappointments and see His appointments.

No journey to recovery is easy, but there is light at the end of the tunnel. The fears, the failures, the frustrations, the disappointments, and the doubts sometimes cloud the light without, but if we keep close to God, His light will illuminate the darkness and bring us safely through. Regardless of the storms that may weather our lives, we do not have to slump into perpetual despair or be angry with God forever. Instead, we can embrace our experiences and view them as opportunities for learning and growth.

> If you will call your troubles experiences and remember that every experience develops some latent force within you, you will grow vigorous and happy, however adverse your circumstances may seem to be. —John Heywood

Today, I am happily married to my husband Dan. I met him at church, and we became good friends. He proved himself to be a true friend and was very helpful to my children. Being in school as a single parent, I found it challenging to divide my time between my children and my studies. That changed when I met Dan. If I had to study, he volunteered to take the children places, allowing me time to complete my studies. If they needed to go to choir rehearsal, club meetings, or anywhere for that matter, he was always there to help. If I had a late class, he would check on them to make sure that they were safe. He became my best friend. What I like the most about him was that each time I told him he was my best friend, he interrupted me with a plea to make the Lord my best friend. He had a firm belief that God should always take precedence in a person's life. Knowing the depths from which I came, I appreciated that. Even though I had already recommitted my life to God and planned never to regress into my old ways, I appreciated the reminder. I will never forget God. He took me out of the depths of despair and led me onto higher ground. He showed me how to be complete and fulfilled in Him. I don't need to seek fulfillment in a person, in a relationship, in a marriage, or in any earthly entity, for my peace and fulfillment is in Him. "And ye are complete in him, which is the head of all principality and power" (Col 2: 10). God fills me with His love, which allows me to love Dan justly. Loving God supremely gives me the opportunity to love Dan rightly. Dan took my children into his care and loved them like any biological father would. My children lacked nothing, and he fought to give them a decent chance in life. I will always love him for that.

When you think that God has failed you, I want you to consider the story of the biblical Naomi, who lost her husband and two sons. Destitute and in despair, she returned to her homeland with her daughter-in-law, Ruth. Naomi must have felt bitter about her situation and bitter toward God. That is why she changed her name to Mara, which means bitter. Little did she know that there is no sorrow, no heartache, no anguish to which our Heavenly Father turns a blind eye. He feels what we feel and is touched by our sorrows. God aligned Naomi and Ruth with the kinsman-redeemer, Boaz, who rescued them from their destitution. Boaz married Ruth, and they became great-grandparents to King David, a seed in the lineage of the Messiah.

Our God can take the most adverse situations and work it out for a good. I want you to also consider the biblical Joseph, who was sold into slavery, lied on by his master's wife, jailed innocently for many years, and whose suffering was prolonged by a broken vow. He, too, must have felt rejected and alone, but God took his bad situation and worked it out for a good. "But as for you, ye thought evil against me; but God meant it unto good, to bring to pass, as it is this day, to save much people alive" (Gen 50: 20).

Sometimes, in our moments of crisis, it is difficult to see the big picture or envision any opportunity for growth, but if we exercise patience and faith in God, we will come out of the experience stronger and better equipped to deal with future crises. The experiences I've endured have added tremendous value to my life. I am a better and stronger person because of them. They have made me more persistent in being the best that I can be. They have helped me to become closer to what I believe is genuinely "me," the me that I was created to be. We never know what lies ahead, but we can trust God to take us through.

Day by Day

Every day, the Lord Himself is near me
With a special mercy for each hour;
All my cares He fain would bear, and cheer me,
He Whose Name is Counselor and Pow'r.
The protection of His child and treasure
Is a charge that on Himself He laid;
"As thy days, thy strength shall be in measure,"
This the pledge to me He made.

—Carolina Sandell Berg

Made in the USA
Columbia, SC
20 June 2022